W0469251

Franz Zach / Rene Gromes

DURCHSTARTEN IN ENGLISCH

ENGLISCH

FÜR DIE 7. SCHULSTUFE

VERITAS
LERNHILFEN

DURCHSTARTEN IN ENGLISCH, Englisch für die 7. Schulstufe

Verfasser: Franz Zach und René Gromes

Verfasser der Durchstartübungen: Do-Ri Amtmann und Kim da Silva

Diesem Lernhilfebuch ist ein Lösungsheft zu den Übungen beigelegt.

Das Buch ist nach der neuen Rechtschreibung abgefasst.

Bibliografische Information Der Deutschen Bibliothek

Die Deutsche Bibliothek verzeichnet diese Publikation in der Deutschen Nationalbibliografie; detaillierte bibliografische Daten sind im Internet über http://dnb.ddb.de abrufbar.

5. Auflage (2004)

Gedruckt in Österreich auf umweltfreundlich hergestelltem Papier

Lektorat: Klaus Kopinitsch

Layout, Herstellung: Kurt Lackner

Illustrationen: Bruno Haberzettl

Umschlagentwurf: Alexander Strohmaier

Satz: Vogel Medien GmbH, Bisamberg

Druck: Landesverlag Druckservice, Linz

ISBN 3-7058-5153-5

INHALTSVERZEICHNIS

Hi! Wir stellen uns vor! 5

Top Ten der Lerntipps 8

Das Zeitwort *(the verb)* 9

present perfect tense (simple and progressive) 9

1. Durchstartübung: Powermudra 19

past tense (simple and progressive) 20
future tense (progressive) 27
past perfect tense 29

2. Durchstartübung: Erdknöpfe und Raumknöpfe 33

Die Leideform *(the passive voice)* 34
Hilfszeitwörter der Aussageweise *(modal verbs)* 45

3. Durchstartübung: Gehirnknöpfe 48

Frage und Verneinung *(question and negation)* 49
Die Zeitstufen – eine Übersicht *(table of tenses and forms)* 61
Kinder, wie die Zeit vergeht – Übungen zu den bekannten Zeiten 63

4. Durchstartübung: Denkmütze 66

Die „if"-Sätze / Bedingungssätze *(if-sentences / conditions)* 67
Die indirekte Rede *(indirect or reported speech)* 74

5. Durchstartübung: Zauberpunkt 93

Das Eigenschaftswort *(the adjective)* 94

Steigerung und Vergleich *(comparison)* 94

6. Durchstartübung: Mudra für den gesunden Willen 107

Das Fürwort *(the pronoun)* 108

Das bezügliche Fürwort *(the relative pronoun)* 108
Das rückbezügliche Fürwort *(the "self"-pronoun)* 117

7. Durchstartübung: Nilpferd 125

Stories 126

8. Durchstartübung: Mudra zum Gehirneinschalten 137

Arbeiten mit dem Wörterbuch *(working with the dictionary)* 138

9. Durchstartübung: Beckenachten und Armkreisen 143

Tests 144

Unregelmäßige Zeitwörter *(irregular verbs)* 156

Versetzung gefährdet – was nun? 159
Aufgaben der Eltern und rechtlicher Rahmen in Deutschland

Nicht genügend! Was können Eltern dagegen tun? 161
Pädagogische Aspekte und rechtliche Situation in Österreich

Stichwortverzeichnis 168

Hi! Wir stellen uns vor!

Kannst du auch von dir behaupten, *"I ♥ ENGLISH"*? Ganz ehrlich und ohne zu flunkern? Vielleicht geht es dir im Augenblick nicht ganz so gut? Du fühlst dich unsicher, deine Noten sind nicht so, wie du sie gern hättest, und vor den *tests* hast du ein wenig Angst? Vielleicht warst du krank und hast Stunden versäumt, und nun gibt es Probleme mit dem Nachlernen? Vielleicht geht dir aber auch in diesem Schuljahr alles zu schnell, und du brauchst mehr Zeit und Gelegenheit zum Nachdenken und Üben?

Das „Durchstarten-Team" will dir helfen, diese Probleme zu meistern, damit du die Frage mit „Ja, natürlich!" oder noch besser mit *"Yes, of course!"* beantworten kannst. Du wirst dabei nicht allein sein: *Maxwell, Mac* und *Charlie* werden dir immer zur Seite stehen. Sie werden dir manchmal sagen, was du tun sollst, und sie wollen dich ganz bestimmt zum Schmunzeln bringen!

Bevor es so richtig losgeht, noch einige Hinweise zur „richtigen" Verwendung von „Durchstarten".

Das Inhaltsverzeichnis sagt dir, worum es in den einzelnen Abschnitten des Buches geht. Es ist übersichtlich gegliedert und durchnummeriert. Der Inhalt deckt den gesamten Lehrstoff der 7. Schulstufe ab.

Das Stichwortverzeichnis am Ende des Buches gibt in alphabetischer Reihenfolge – von *active voice* bis Zukunft – alle wichtigen Stichwörter mit Seitenangabe an, sodass du schnell findest, wonach du suchst.

Alle Kapitel sind gleich aufgebaut. Zuerst kommt eine Erklärung, die du gründlich und genau durcharbeiten sollst. Dann folgen viele abwechslungsreiche Übungen. Jede Übung beginnt mit einem Beispiel *(example).* Du kannst dabei sofort erkennen, was du in der Folge selbst tun sollst.

Zu „Durchstarten" gibt es ein **Lösungsheft.** Du sollst es aber nur zum Vergleichen und Verbessern deiner Antworten verwenden, nachdem du die Übungen selbständig erarbeitet hast. Denke daran: „Wer mogelt, belügt sich selbst!"

Die *tests* sind im Schwierigkeitsgrad und im Inhalt auf den Lehrplan der 7. Schulstufe abgestimmt. Eine Punktetabelle erlaubt dir, deine Arbeit zu bewerten und selbst zu benoten. *Good luck!*

Die Symbole in der Randspalte sind Signale. Sie wollen dich auf wichtige Dinge aufmerksam machen oder dir sagen, was du tun sollst.

Los geht's. Eine Übung *(exercise)* ist angesagt.

Aha! So geht das!

Achtung! Die Sache ist verdammt wichtig. Lieber noch einmal durchdenken.

Eine Sprachregel, die du auf jeden Fall beherrschen solltest.

Mac hat einen Tipp für dich im Sinne von „So kannst du dir das merken" oder „So geht's leichter".

Da hilft nur eins: Auswendiglernen!

Es wird ernst! Am Ende eines Stoffgebietes gibt es einen Wettbewerb mit Punkteauswertung und Beurteilung. Diese Übung zeigt dir, ob du schon am Ziel bist oder noch eine Runde (Wiederholung) benötigst.

Take it easy! Ruh dich aus, mach später/morgen weiter. Es ist schließlich sinnvoller, an mehreren Tagen 30 Minuten zu üben, statt an einem Tag alles machen zu wollen. Übrigens: Hast du ein Kapitel beendet, solltest du ebenfalls eine Pause machen, auch wenn dich kein Symbol daran erinnert.

Die ***stories*** sollen dir nicht nur Freude am Lesen bereiten, sondern auch Hilfe im Umgang mit Texten sein. Hier kannst du lernen und üben, wie man Fragen sinnvoll stellt und beantwortet und wie man kurze und einfache Geschichten zusammenfasst oder nacherzählt.

Du selbst entscheidest, wie du mit dem Buch arbeitest. Du kannst es vom Anfang bis zum Schluss „durchackern", oder du konzentrierst dich auf das Kapitel, das du gerade nachlernen willst oder musst. Gleichgültig wofür du dich entscheidest: Lerne regelmäßig und langsam, damit das Gelernte auch „sitzt"! Hektisches „Pauken" oder „Strebern" knapp vor einem *test* verwirrt und schadet meist mehr, als es nützt.

Aber das ist eigentlich schon ein Tipp, wie man richtig lernt. **Lerntipps** findest du auf der folgenden Seite. Das kann manchmal mehr helfen, als das Lernen für Englisch selbst.

Wir möchten dir auch noch eine andere Möglichkeit zeigen, deinen Lernerfolg zu steigern. Das Lernen wird dir damit garantiert leichter fallen, vorausgesetzt du tust mit und übst regelmäßig. Das Ganze beruht auf folgender Erkenntnis: Steigere die Energie deines Körpers, und du steigerst deine Leistungsfähigkeit und damit auch deine Lernleistung. Erlaubtes Doping sozusagen!

Das Tolle daran: Du schaffst das mit einfachen Bewegungsübungen. Wir nennen sie **„Durchstartübungen".** Sie bringen dich so richtig auf Touren. Sie ermöglichen dir, dass du in kurzer Zeit mehr begreifst und dein Wissen bei einer Prüfung auch zur Verfügung hast. Lerngymnastik macht durstig. Genehmige dir vor und nach den Übungen ein Glas Wasser.

Das „Durchstarten-Team" wünscht dir „Gutes Gelingen" und Freude bei der Arbeit mit dem Buch, damit sich der Erfolg bald einstellt. Wir wünschen uns, dass du bald sagen kannst:

„YES, I ♥ ENGLISH!"

TOP TEN DER LERNTIPPS

Diese zehn Punkte solltest du beim Lernen beachten:

1. Zeitplan. Trage in einen Kalender alle **Prüfungstermine** ein. Markiere die Tage, die du zum Lernen vor einer Prüfung brauchst. Das schafft Überblick.

2. Stoffübersicht. Erstelle eine **Liste der** einzelnen **Prüfungsgebiete**, lasse daneben Platz zum Abhaken. Das spornt dich an und gibt dir Übersicht.

3. Entspannen. Beginne nicht sofort nach der Schule mit den Aufgaben. Eine einstündige **Entspannungspause** fördert deine Konzentration.

4. Arbeitsplatz. Richte dir einen eigenen Arbeitsplatz ein. Auf diesem **ordne übersichtlich** deine Unterlagen.

5. Aufwärmen. Verwende dazu unsere Durchstartübungen. **Lerngymnastik** steigert deinen Lernerfolg. Außerdem bist du damit deinen Mitschülern um die berühmte Nasenlänge voraus.

6. Strukturieren. Was du gliederst, kannst du besser behalten. **Markiere** Wesentliches **bunt**, mache dir am Rand Notizen.

7. Pausen. Nach 30 bis 45 Minuten Lernen lässt deine Konzentration nach. Lege daher eine etwa **10 Minuten** lange Pause ein. In der Pause mache eine Durchstartübung. Nach der Pause schreibst du eine nicht besonders anstrengende Hausaufgabe. Dann erst lernst du weiter. Auch **dein Gehirn liebt** die **Abwechslung**.

8. Motivieren. Jeden Tag nach dem Lernen sollte es etwas geben, worauf du dich **freuen** kannst (spielen, ins Kino gehen . . .).

9. Wiederholen. Beim Wiederholen festigst du den Stoff. Ein heißer Tipp: **Abendwiederholung**. Das Gehirn lernt weiter, während du schon schläfst. Das funktioniert aber nur, wenn du nach der Abendwiederholung dein Gehirn mit nichts anderem mehr belästigst.

10. Prüfung. Wenn du ängstlich bist, **„spiele"** zu Hause **Prüfung**. Das macht selbstbewusster, und du gehst gestärkt zur echten Prüfung.

DAS ZEITWORT

THE VERB

present perfect tense
simple form and progressive form

Present perfect tense – manchmal auch „Vergangenheit" genannt – zählt zu den schwierigsten Punkten der englischen Grammatik. Wir fangen aber mit dem Einfachen an und arbeiten uns zum Schwierigen vor!

present perfect simple

- ☆ wird mit ***have / has*** + ***past participle*** (3. Grundform) gebildet;
- ☆ beschreibt **abgeschlossene Handlungen und Zustände,** die aber **Auswirkungen und Folgen auf das „Hier und Jetzt"** haben;
- ☆ steht (fast) **immer ohne Zeitangabe,** da nicht der Zeitpunkt der Handlung, sondern ihre Auswirkungen und Folgen wichtig sind;
- ☆ steht **immer** in einem **Zusammenhang mit der Gegenwart *(present tense)***; daher auch der Name ***present*** *perfect;*
- ☆ steht **nie** in einem **Zusammenhang mit *past tense*** (denn *past tense* bezeichnet immer Handlungen, die in der Vergangenheit geschehen sind, und sagt nichts über Auswirkungen und Folgen auf das „Hier und Jetzt" aus).

Erinnere dich: **So wird *present perfect simple* gebildet**.

I	have	been	to London many times. I think it's great.
You	have	taken	my pen. Put it back, please!
He	has	sent	us some catalogues. Let's look at them.
She	has	gone	shopping to town. She is not at home.
It	has	begun	to rain. Let's call a taxi.
We	have	had	enough to eat now, thank you.
You	have	talked	to Sandy. Will she be at the party?
They	have	started	a fight. Let's call Mr Latimer.

So einfach werden Frage und Verneinung gebildet:

☆ Bei der Frage vertauschst du **Subjekt** und ***have/has***.
You have *seen my pen.* → ***Have you*** *seen my pen?*

☆ Bei der Verneinung folgt auf ***have/has*** sofort ***not***.
*I **have not** been to London this year.*
*It **has not** begun to rain yet. Let's go outside.*

1

Bilde *present perfect simple* mit den angegebenen Personen und Verben.

1. You (write) a wonderful story, Daniel!
2. The children (build) a big snowman in the garden.
3. Charlie (find) Maxwell's old shoes.
4. I (wait) long enough. I'm going home now.
5. (you, see) "Streetfigther" yet? It's very exciting.
6. (Ted, bring) back our basketball? I'd like to play now.
7. We can still catch the bus. It (not leave) yet.
8. I (not talk) to Mr Bean yet, but I'll talk to him soon.

present perfect simple oder ***past simple***?

Die Entscheidung ist für uns Deutschsprechende nicht einfach! In unserer Sprache macht es nicht viel Unterschied, ob wir

„Vater **flog** nach Paris" oder „Vater **ist** nach Paris **geflogen**" sagen.

Im Englischen geht das nicht so einfach, da *past simple* und *present perfect simple* einfach etwas anderes bedeuten!

☆ ***past simple**: "Father **flew** to Paris."*

heißt, dass er irgendwann einmal in die französische Hauptstadt geflogen ist und vielleicht schon seit langem wieder zurück ist. Meist steht bei solchen Angaben auch, wann das geschah. Also etwa: *". . . **last week**."*

☆ ***present perfect simple:** "Father **has flown** to Paris."*

heißt, dass seine Reise eine Auswirkung auf das „Hier und Jetzt" hat, nämlich diese: Vater ist nicht da, er ist in Frankreich! Wir erfahren nicht, wann er abflog, und das will uns der Sprecher auch gar nicht mitteilen. Er will uns bloß sagen, warum sein Vater nicht da ist.

Glücklicherweise gibt es verschiedene **Reizwörter,** die auf diese zwei Zeitstufen hinweisen:

A

für ***past simple***	für ***present perfect simple***
yesterday .... gestern	***yet*** ..... schon, bereits (in Fragen)
last *(week)* .... letzte, vorige	***not yet*** .... noch nicht
in *(1993)* .... im Jahr (1993)	***just*** .... soeben, gerade (eben)
on *(May 1)* .... am (1. Mai)	***Look! Listen!*** ... (als Hinweis auf Folgen oder Auswirkungen)
(a year) ***ago*** ...... vor (einem Jahr)	***so far*** .... bisher, bis jetzt/heute
when *(he came)* ...... als (er kam)	***since, for*** .... seit
	already .... schon, bereits

2 *Present perfect simple* (reicht bis zum „Hier und Jetzt") oder *past simple* (in der Vergangenheit angesiedelt)? Setze die richtige Form des Verbs ein.

1. Uncle Angus (read) many books about Scotland. He is really an expert.
2. (anybody, see) Colin? I can't find him anywhere.
3. Why (you, not wake) me up yesterday? – I (forget).
4. Yesterday Tim and I (go) to the cinema. It (be) great.
5. What a surprise! Linda and Ron (get) married!
6. My parents (get) married in 1981. That (be) seventeen years ago.

present perfect progressive

- beschreibt **Handlungen,** die zu einem **vergangenen Zeitpunkt begonnen** haben und im **Augenblick des Sprechens** (Gegenwart) noch immer **andauern** und noch **nicht abgeschlossen** sind;
- stellt somit den **unmittelbaren Zusammenhang** zwischen **Vergangenheit und Gegenwart** her;
- steht (fast) immer mit der **(Zeit-)Angabe „seit . . ."** (engl. *since / for*)

- **So wird *present perfect progressive* gebildet:**

I	have	been	standing	here since 6 o'clock. I'm tired.
You	have	been	looking	at me for twenty minutes. What's wrong?
He	has	been	running	up and down the street for half an hour.
She	has	been	waiting	since early this morning. She must be cold.
It	has	been	snowing	for a week. All the roads are closed.
We	have	been	planning	our holiday in Australia for over a year.
You	have	been	helping	us since I can remember. Thank you!
They	have	been	practising	for the big ball. Now they dance wonderfully.

Frage und Verneinung bereiten auch hier keine Schwierigkeiten:

☆ Bei der Frage vertauschst du **Subjekt** und ***have / has***:

It ***has*** *been snowing since Monday.*
Since when ***has it*** *been snowing?*

☆ Die Verneinung kommt bei *present perfect progressive* höchst selten vor. Solltest du dennoch irgendwann einmal auf sie stoßen, dann merke dir: Auf *have / has* folgt sofort *not,* genauso wie bei *present perfect simple.*

3

Bilde *present perfect progressive* mit den angegebenen Verben und Personen.

1. You (sit) here with your friends for half an hour.
   Do some work now!
2. How long (the boys, play) football? –
   For an hour or so.
3. I (write) "Thank You" notes for three hours.
4. Since when (you, look) for your ticket? –
   Since this morning.
5. They (work) on this bridge for five years.
   It's still not finished.
6. Charlie (wait) for Susi since eleven o'clock.

Das große **Problem** für uns Deutschsprechende **mit *present perfect progressive*** liegt darin, dass es etwas Vergleichbares in unserer Sprache gar nicht gibt! Auf Deutsch sind das die **„schon seit . . ."-Sätze,** und die stehen in der Gegenwart. Merke dir also:

Immer wenn du in einem Satz auf ***"since"*** oder ***"for"*** in der Bedeutung von **„schon seit"** triffst, sollte eine Alarmglocke läuten: ***present perfect progressive* und nicht *present tense*!**

since* oder *for

Beide bedeuten auf Deutsch **„seit"**, aber

since sagt, **ab wann** eine Handlung schon andauert (Zeitpunkt, Jahreszahl, Tag, Ereignis . . .);
for sagt, **wie lange schon** eine Handlung andauert (Zeitspanne; ein paar Stunden, Tage oder Wochen, . . .).

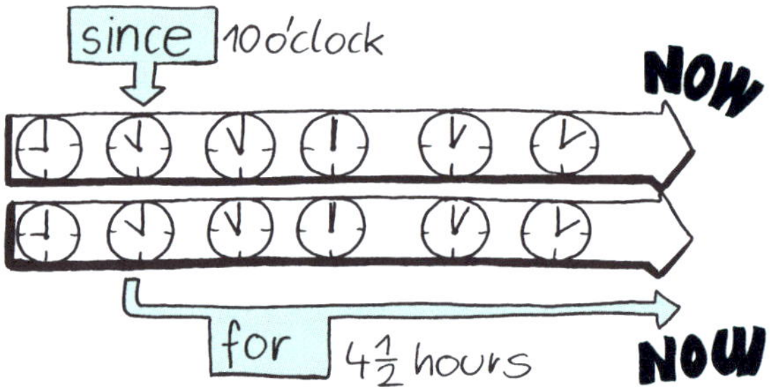

4 Setze *since* oder *for* vor die folgenden Zeitangaben.

example: Christmas Day → since Christmas Day
a long time → for a long time

1. six o'clock
2. 1992
3. nine months
4. I came to this town
5. six hours
6. twenty minutes
7. your birthday
8. a very long time

5 Übersetze die folgenden Sätze. Beachte die Warnung von Seite 13 und den Unterschied zwischen *since* und *for*!

1. Wir wohnen schon seit vielen Jahren hier. *(live)*
2. Onkel Albert arbeitet schon seit fünf Jahren in England.
3. Ich lerne schon seit zweieinhalb Jahren Englisch. *(study)*
4. Du liegst schon seit 10 Uhr in der Sonne. *(lie)*
5. Ich denke schon seit Tagen über diese Frage nach. *(think about)*
6. Jack und Maria tanzen schon seit dem Beginn der Party miteinander. *(dance with each other)*
7. Dieses Haus steht schon seit dem Mittelalter hier. *(the Middle Ages)*
8. Wir üben *present perfect tense* schon seit einer Woche. *(practise)*

Selbstverständlich gibt es auch **„Ausnahmen"** von der Regel (sonst wär's ja nicht *"typically English"*!). Damit sind die **Zeitwörter** gemeint, die normalerweise **nicht in *progressive form*** vorkommen!

Zur Erinnerung und Ergänzung eine alphabetische Liste der wichtigsten **Zeitwörter, die für gewöhnlich nur in *simple form* stehen.** Du solltest sie dir im Lauf der Zeit – *the sooner, the better* – gut einprägen und sie auch des Öfteren wiederholen, damit du nicht aus der Übung kommst!

A

be	sein, sich befinden	***mean***	bedeuten
believe	glauben	***need***	brauchen
belong	gehören	***prefer***	bevorzugen
forget	vergessen	***realise***	erkennen
hate	hassen	***remember***	sich erinnern
hear	hören	***see***	sehen
know	kennen, wissen	***seem***	scheinen
like	mögen, gerne tun	***understand***	verstehen
love	lieben, sehr gerne tun	***want***	wollen

„Ich **kenne** Martha **schon seit** vielen Jahren."

heißt daher weder: *"I am knowing Martha for many years."*
noch: *"I know Martha for many years."*
und auch nicht: *"I have been knowing Martha for many years."*

sondern: *"I **have known** Martha for many years."*

6

Hier geht es nur um *present perfect*! Du entscheidest, ob *simple* oder *progressive* stimmt. Denke daran: Bei *simple form* weißt du nur, dass etwas geschehen ist, weil du die Auswirkungen und Folgen siehst oder spürst; du weißt nicht, wann es passiert ist. Bei *progressive form* weißt du, wie lange (seit wann) eine Handlung schon andauert. Beachte aber auch die „Ausnahmen"!

examples: Hey, someone (put) a notice on our front door! →
Hey, someone **has put** a notice on our front door!

(Das geschah irgendwann, während wir weg waren, und „hier und jetzt" sehen wir die Folgen = den Zettel an der Eingangstür!)

I (play) the violin for two hours. →
I **have been playing** the violin for two hours.

(Ich spiele schon seit zwei Stunden; das heißt, ich habe vor zwei Stunden damit begonnen und spiele „hier und jetzt" noch immer!)

1. Tanya (work) here since April, but she does not like it.
2. Look, it (rain)! The streets are wet.
3. Mr Rendell (teach) English for fifteen years.
4. Somebody (smoke) a cigar in this room. I can smell it.
5. How do you like my room now? I (paint) it yellow and white.
6. I can come on the bike tour with you. Dad (repair) my bike.
7. Mike is a good hockey player. He (play) for only five minutes and he (already, score) two goals. (to score a goal = ein Tor schießen)
8. Look! Someone (kick) a ball through the window!
9. Lockwood Castle (belong) to the same family since the 14th century.
10. My dad (want) to make a holiday in Canada since I can remember.
11. How long (you, know) about Jenny's accident? – Since Saturday.
12. Francis and I (be) in the same scout group for two years.

Überprüfe deine Antworten mit Hilfe des Lösungsheftes. Wenn du (fast) alle Beispiele richtig gelöst hast (bis zu zwei Fehler sind erlaubt), kannst du dich getrost an die Punkteübung heranwagen! Sie enthält die gleiche Art von Aufgaben wie *exercises* 2 und 6.

1

Setze die angegebenen Zeitwörter in die richtige Zeitstufe. In Frage kommen *past simple, present perfect simple* und *present perfect progressive.*

❍❍ 1. Tim (write) six pages of his book this morning. Here they are. Yesterday he (write) only five pages.

❍ 2. Let's play tennis! – No, thanks. I (already, play) three matches this week and I need a rest.

❍❍ 3. Paul (make) films since he was in High School. This year he (make) two very good films about southern Germany. One of them is on TV tonight.

❍❍ 4. Our neighbours (travel) around Europe for three months. They (be) to twelve countries so far.

❍ 5. I'm sorry, dad is not here. He (just, leave) for work.

❍❍ 6. (you, find) your passport yet, Joe? – No! I (look) for it for two hours but I can't find it anywhere.

❍ 7. Nancy and Bob (get) married five years ago.

❍❍ 8. Chuck, (you, be) able to find an answer to exercise 7? – No, not yet, but I (think) about it for days.

❍ 9. (anybody, hear) from Carl? – I have! He is in London at the moment.

❍ 10. Don't forget to tidy up your room, Jack! – I (already, do) it, dad.

❍ 11. Would you like something to drink, Sally? – No, thanks, I (just, have) a cup of tea.

❍❍❍ 12. How many goals (you, score) this season, Graham? – Only two, but we (play) only three games so far. – And last year? How many goals (you, score) last season? – Twenty-one!

❍ 13. Good news! Monica (have) a baby! They're going to call him Simon.

❍ 14. Go to bed now, Danny! You (watch) TV for more than four hours. That's really enough.

21 oder 20 Punkte: ***Perfect!*** 19 bis 17 Punkte: ***More practice will make you perfect!*** 16 bis 14 Punkte: ***Far from perfect!*** 13 und darunter: ***Let's not talk about it for the moment!*** Aber im Ernst – du musst das alles noch gründlicher üben! Doch egal, wie das Ergebnis aussieht: Du hast dir eine ausgiebige Pause redlich verdient!

HALLO IHR MÜDEN KRIEGER!
WENN IHR WOLLT, ZAUBERE ICH EUCH MIT EIN PAAR LUSTIGEN ÜBUNGEN WIEDER FIT!!
?
WAS IST MIT MEINER LIMO-DOSE LOS?

POWERMUDRA

Müde? Erschöpft? Verzweifelt?
Das Powermudra gibt dir Kraft für deine Aufgaben:

Du legst Daumen und Ringfingerkuppen zusammen und den Zeigefinger auf das erste Daumengelenk.
Du kannst es auch nur mit rechter oder linker Hand halten.
Dauer der Übung: mindestens 3 Minuten. Führe das Powermudra mindestens 6-mal täglich durch.

Stell dir einmal vor,
du bist Besitzer eines tollen Autos. Es kann schnell fahren, es bringt dich gut und sicher an jedes von dir gewünschte Ziel. Du braust gerade auf der Autobahn dahin, aber plötzlich stottert der Motor. Du drückst stärker aufs Gaspedal, trotzdem wird dein Auto immer langsamer und bleibt sogar stehen. Du kannst nun schimpfen, einen Kopfstand machen, das Auto neu lackieren, die Mitfahrer rausschmeißen – das Auto wird sich keinen Zentimeter bewegen. Wenn dein Auto keinen Treibstoff mehr hat, kannst du tun, was du willst. Du musst das Richtige tun: **TANKEN!** Dann kannst du deine Fahrt fortsetzen und kommst ans Ziel.

Ebenso ist es mit deiner eigenen Kraft. Wenn deine Energie zu niedrig ist, hast du es sehr schwer, eine gute Lernleistung zu erbringen. Von leicht und locker zu schaffen, was Lehrer und Eltern von dir fordern, ganz zu schweigen.
Unlust, Müdigkeit, Ärger oder Verzweiflung breiten sich in deinem Körper aus. Sie zehren an deiner Energie. Wie willst du aber eine Leistung bringen, wenn dein Tank leer ist?

Daher heißt's auftanken mit dem Powermudra!

past tense

past tense simple form

Past simple ist die „normale" Erzählzeit. Du verwendest sie, wenn du über vergangene Ereignisse erzählst. Meist reihst du dabei ein Ereignis an das andere, wie im folgenden Beispiel. Charlie erzählt:

> *This morning I **got** up at 7 o'clock. I **went** to the bathroom and **cleaned** my teeth. Then I **put** on my jogging suit and **did** some warming-up exercises. My friend Mac **came** and together we **jogged** around the park for about twenty minutes. Back home I **took** a shower and **prepared** breakfast. I **had** toast and tea. After that . . .*

Gezeichnet sieht das dann so aus:

past tense progressive form

Past progressive (oder auch ***past continuous*** oder ***past expanded***) sieht aus wie folgt:
At 4 o'clock this afternoon . . .

I	***was***	***watching***	*TV.*	*we*	***were***	***playing***	*cards.*
you	***were***	***taking***	*a walk.*				
he	***was***	***driving***	*home.*	*they*	***were***	***packing***	*their bags.*

"He ***was driving*** *home from work"* bedeutet, dass ein Mann **zu einem bestimmten Zeitpunkt irgendwann in der Vergangenheit** gerade mit seinem Auto nach Hause unterwegs war. Die eigentliche **Handlung** war zu diesem bestimmten Zeitpunkt *(at 4 o'clock this afternoon)* **noch nicht beendet.** → *He was in the middle of doing something.*

I/he/she/it | was + play**ing**
you/we/they | were + watch**ing**

Sehen wir uns an, welche Möglichkeiten es zur Festlegung des bestimmten Zeitpunktes gibt:

1 eine genaue Zeitangabe:

→ *What were you doing* ***yesterday between 11 and 12 o'clock****?*
(Yesterday at 11 a. m.) Charlie and I ***were standing*** *in front of Buckingham Palace. We* ***were waiting*** *for the Changing of the Guard.*

7

Hier findest du eine Aufstellung einiger Dinge, die James gestern erledigt hat, verbunden mit einer Zeittabelle. Du sollst mit Hilfe der Tabelle sagen, was James zu einem bestimmten Zeitpunkt gemacht hat.

examples: At 6:45 a.m. James **was jogging** in the park.
At 10 a.m. James **was working** in the office.

6:30–7:00 jogging in the park	9:00–12:30 worked in the office
7:05–7:10 took a shower	12:45–1:15 had lunch
7:15–7:30 had breakfast	1:30–5:00 worked in the office
7:40–7:50 waited for his train	5:30–6:00 went home by train
8:00–8:30 read the newspaper	6:30–7:15 played football with son

1. At 7:08 a.m. . . .
2. At 7:25 a.m. . . .
3. At 7:45 a.m. . . .
4. At 8:20 a.m. . . .
5. At 1 p.m. . . .
6. At 3:30 p.m. . . .
7. At 5.45 p.m. . . .
8. At 7 p.m. . . .

2 ein Ereignis, das während der Handlung eintritt
(„kurze Handlung unterbricht längere Handlung")

→ *Dad was driving home from work*
when he had a flat.

→ *We were playing cards*
when the lights suddenly went out.

R Die längere Handlung (das Nachhausefahren, das Kartenspielen) hatte schon früher begonnen und war zu dem bestimmten Zeitpunkt (Reifenpanne, kein Licht; das heißt, als die kürzere Handlung dazukam) noch nicht abgeschlossen.

Sicher ist dir aufgefallen, dass der Gliedsatz, der den bestimmten Zeitpunkt bezeichnet, oft mit ***when*** = „als" eingeleitet wird.

. . . when the light went out. → . . . als das Licht ausging.
. . . when he had a flat. → . . . als er eine Reifenpanne hatte.

8 Was geschah in dem Augenblick, als dieses „Foto" geschossen wurde? Schau dir das Bild gut an und bilde Sätze mit *past progressive.* Beginne mit *"When I took this photo, . . ."*

example: When I took this photo, Peggy was jumping into the pool.

1. Kevin – run into the garage
2. Sue – come out of the garage
3. a man – sell ice-cream
4. Sammy – drive his "Formula One" car down the street
5. a mouse – cross the street in front of the ice-cream cart
6. "Bonzo" – chase (= jagen) the neighbour's cat
7. a bird – fly over the house
8. a squirrel – climb up the tree

Lies dir die folgenden Sätze gut durch und überlege, ob sie das Gleiche oder Verschiedenes aussagen.

Mike was running down the hill ***when*** *he fell and broke his arm.*
(Er lief den Hügel hinunter, als er stürzte und . . .)
While *Mike was running down the hill, he fell and broke his arm.*
(**Als / Während** er den Hügel hinunterlief, stürzte er und . . .)

Wenn du findest, dass die zwei Sätze das Gleiche aussagen, hast du Recht! Man muss somit nicht jeden Satz nach „demselben Muster stricken", sondern man kann Abwechslung in den grauen Alltag der Sprache bringen.

In dieser Übung wird der „bestimmte Zeitpunkt" nicht durch eine Uhrzeit, sondern durch ein hinzutretendes Ereignis („kürzere Handlung") bestimmt. Du sollst zunächst *past simple* und *past progressive* richtig einsetzen und in einem zweiten Schritt die Sätze „umformulieren" (das heißt, *while* statt *when* und umgekehrt).

example: I (play) the drums when mum (bring) me some tea. →
I was playing the drums when mum brought me some tea. →
While I was playing the drums mum brought me some tea.

1. Everybody (sleep) when a burglar (= Einbrecher) (break) into the house.
2. While Sandra (watch) a love film on TV, she (fall) asleep.
3. Uncle Harry (wait) for his train when he (find) a wallet on the platform.
4. While dad (cook) dinner, he (drop) the pan and (burn) himself.
5. I (take) pictures of Trafalgar Square when a pickpocket (try) to steal my wallet.
6. Thousands of people (watch) the open-air concert when a thunderstorm (break) out.
7. While Gina (look) at the dresses in the shop window, a tourist (ask) her the way to the Science Museum.
8. While Sylvia (copy) my maths homework, Mr Jenkins, our maths teacher, (come) into the classroom.

3 eine (längere) Handlung, die gleichzeitig abläuft:

→ *I was listening to the radio* ***while I was driving home from work.***

Hier wird der Zeitpunkt, zu dem diese Handlungen geschahen, gar nicht mehr wirklich genannt. Wir wissen nur, dass sie **irgendwann in der Vergangenheit** begonnen haben (nicht unbedingt zur gleichen Zeit) und eine Zeit lang „nebeneinander" oder „parallel" abliefen.

Sehr oft wird dieses „Nebeneinander" durch ***while*** **= während** ausgedrückt:
. . . while I was driving home.
. . . während ich nach Hause fuhr.
While I was taking a shower . . .
Während ich mich duschte . . .

In diesen Fällen verwendest du

10 Mehrere längere Handlungen (nur *past progressive*) oder ein bestimmter Zeitpunkt (*past simple* für das Ereignis, *past progressive* für die längere Handlung)?

1. While Susi (take) pictures of the birds at Trafalgar Square, the birds (watch) her.
2. What (you, do) while I (look) for my keys?
3. I (walk) home from my tennis lesson when it (begin) to rain.
4. When I (meet) Bill for the first time, he (live) in Arizona.
5. Who (look) out of the window when the accident (happen)?
6. While I (have) lunch, mum and dad (get) the car ready.
7. While I (walk) home from my tennis lesson, it (begin) to rain.
8. Last night I (watch) a thriller on TV when someone (knock) at the door.

1

Past simple or progressive? Überlege und setze die richtige Form ein. Es geht um die *big points*!

❍❍ 1. Columbus (try) to find a route to India when he (find) America.
❍❍ 2. Ronny's father (hurt) his back yesterday while he (plant) a tree.
❍❍ 3. While Mabel (lie) in bed with a fever, she (think) of her next summer holidays.
❍❍ 4. It (rain) when our plane (land) at Heathrow Airport.
❍❍ 5. But the sun (come) out again while we (wait) for a taxi to our hotel.
❍❍ 6. Did you hear? Daniel (have) an accident while he (drive) home
❍❍ from work. – Yes, I know. But when I last (see) him, he (work) again as usual.
❍❍❍ 7. I (not go) very fast on my bike when I (slip) and (fall). While I
❍❍❍ (sit) there, my neighbour (come) and (offer) to drive me home in his car.

20 and 19 *points:* ***very nice***; 18 und 17: ***nice***; 16 und 15 ***okay, but . . .***

PAUSE

2

Nur für Experten! Du findest hier einen kurzen, zusammenhängenden Text, in den du die richtigen Zeitwortformen einsetzen sollst. Es heißt wieder: *past simple or past progressive*!

❍❍ When I (get) . . . up at 5:30 on Saturday morning, the sun (shine) . . .
❍❍ and the birds (sing) . . . . It (be) . . . a lovely day.
❍❍ I (take) . . . my rucksack, (put) . . . some pieces of bread and cheese
❍ and an apple in it and (leave) . . . the hotel in the mountains where I
❍❍ (stay) . . . for the weekend. In the lobby of the hotel I (wait) . . . for
❍❍ my friend Charlie, who (stay) . . . at the hotel, too. While I (wait) . . . , I
❍ (watch) . . . the early morning news on TV. A nice young woman (say)
❍ . . . that the weather would be fine all weekend.
❍❍ When Charlie (arrive) . . . , we (start) . . . on our tour of the mountain
❍ behind the hotel. After half an hour of walking we (meet) . . . two
❍ tourists, a man and a woman, who (go) . . . in the same direction
❍❍ (= Richtung) as we. Charlie (ask) . . . them if they (want) . . . to come
❍❍ with us, and they (say) . . . yes. So we (walk) . . . on together.
❍❍ They (be) . . . very nice, and we (have) . . . a lot of fun.

Das war wohl nicht ganz so leicht, oder? Daher sind wir bei der Punktevergabe etwas großzügiger: Ab 20 Richtigen kannst du **stolz** auf dich sein. Von 19 bis 14 ist's auch **noch okay**. 13 und 12 Punkte sind **noch positiv,** aber bei 11 und noch weniger empfehlen Mac und Charlie noch einen **Wiederholungsdurchgang** ab Seite 20!

Die Zukunft

future progressive

Future progressive verwendest du für **eine Handlung,** die zu einem bestimmten Zeitpunkt in der Zukunft stattfinden wird.

Einige Beispiele sollen das genauer zeigen:

→ *At this time next month Cathy and Jim **will be driving** through Spain.*
(Nächsten Monat um diese Zeit werden sie gerade durch Spanien fahren.)
→ *At this time tomorrow you **will be laughing** about this silly mistake.*
→ *At 7 o'clock on Sunday morning we **will be sleeping.***
→ *At 4 p.m. next Monday **I'll be playing** in the finals. I'm very nervous!*

Die Bildung von *future progressive* ist recht einfach und für alle Personen gleich:

I, you, he, she, it, we, they ***will be + present participle***
(selten findet man bei ***I*** und ***we*** statt *will* auch noch ***shall***)

Frage und Verneinung werden mit ***will*** gebildet.

At this time tomorrow we will be lying on the beach. →

Will we be lying on the beach at this time tomorrow?
Who will be lying on the beach at this time tomorrow?
Where will we be lying at this time tomorrow?
When will we be lying on the beach?
What will we be doing at this time tomorrow?
We will not (won't) be lying on the beach at this time tomorrow.

11 Bilde mit den folgenden Sätzen alle Fragen und Verneinungen.

1. At five o'clock Tim will be playing billiards at Jack's place. (5+1)
2. A week from today Maria and I will be sitting on a train for Paris. (4+1)
3. The guns will be firing a salute when the Queen arrives. (4+1)

12 Stell dir vor, für morgen Nachmittag ist Schönwetter angesagt, und alle freuen sich schon auf draußen. Was werden sie morgen um diese Zeit tun? Schau dir die Zeichnung an und bilde Sätze mit *future progressive.* Stelle dir dabei jedesmal (im Stillen) die Frage: *"What will . . . be doing at this time tomorrow?"*

example: Susi – fish in the pond →
(At this time tomorrow) Susi **will be fishing** in the pond.

1. Alfred – play with his toy train
2. Mac – listen to the radio
3. Maxwell – fix the roof of the tree house
4. Charlie – read a love story
5. Donald – try to sell some lemonade
6. Doris – mow the lawn (= den Rasen mähen)
7. Father – plant a tree
8. Billy Joe – ride her pony

Die Vorvergangenheit (das Plusquamperfekt)

Die **Bildung** von *past perfect tense* ist recht einfach und für alle Personen der Ein- und Mehrzahl gleich:

R

past perfect tense = had + past participle (3. Grundform)

Mit Hilfe von *past perfect tense* sagst du, **welche von mindestens zwei vergangenen Handlungen früher als die andere(n) geschehen ist.** Die frühere Handlung ist dabei völlig abgeschlossen, wenn die spätere beginnt.

*I **had read** the book before I saw the film.*

↓	↓
frühere Handlung	spätere Handlung
↓	↓
past perfect tense	*past tense*

(Du könntest die zwei Handlungen natürlich auch in ihrer richtigen Reihenfolge anführen und sagen:

I read the book first. Then I saw the film. = zweimal *past tense*)

13

Setze das Zeitwort in der Klammer in *past perfect tense.*

example: Mary (give) me Tony's address before she left. →
Mary **had given** me Tony's address before she left.

1. When the boys arrived at the cinema, the film (already, start).
2. Before we reached the station we saw that we (lose) our way.
3. All the tickets (be) sold before the concert began.
4. They took a shower after they (finish) the game.
5. I asked Mr Green how many books he (read).
6. Mum asked me why I (not tidy up) my room.
7. Bob was sorry that he (told) me the story.
8. Alan watched TV after he (have) lunch.

Vergleiche deine Lösungen mit dem Lösungsheft. Nur wenn du (fast) alle richtig hast, „darfst" du weitermachen.

14

Jedes der folgenden Beispiele beschreibt Handlungen, die irgendwann einmal in der Vergangenheit stattfanden und die abgeschlossen sind. Eine davon fand vor der anderen statt; sie steht in *past perfect tense,* die spätere Handlung steht in *past tense.* Schau dir die Sache also gut an und kombiniere logisch!

example: I met George in the city. Then we went to a café. →
After I **had met** George in the city, we **went** to a café.

1. Mum read the letter. Then she told us that Aunt Liz was coming.
2. I helped the lady with the shopping. Then she gave me £ 1.
3. Fred finished the letter. Then he posted (= aufgeben) it.
4. Henry came home. Then Mary wanted to talk to him.
5. Catherine put on some make-up. Then she went out.
6. We left the cinema. Then we went to a restaurant.
7. Dad had his breakfast. Then he drove to work.
8. Mary went home. Then I told Peter about her.

Setze die Verben in Klammer in *past perfect tense.* Du kannst dabei gleichzeitig die *irregular verbs* üben.

example: The teacher asked me which colour I (choose). →
The teacher asked me which colour I had chosen.

- ❍ 1. Peter ran home after a dog (bite) him.
- ❍ 2. Litte Joey went to his mum after he (build) the sandcastle.
- ❍ 3. Molly, our cat, ate the mouse after she (catch) it.
- ❍ 4. Steven showed me the picture he (draw).
- ❍ 5. The coach asked me why I (not throw) the ball to Mike.
- ❍ 6. The woman told the doctor that she (feel) worse the day before.
- ❍ 7. We looked out of the window after the bird (fly) away.
- ❍ 8. I was sure that nobody (show) me the photos before.
- ❍ 9. Dad asked me why I (not wake) him up earlier.
- ❍ 10. Linda told me that she (already, drive) her father's car.

Du brauchst schon 10 Richtige
für ein ***very good***!

Wenn du mit den *irregular verbs* Probleme hast, dann wiederhole sie gründlich. Ohne sie kannst du *past perfect tense* nicht richtig bilden.

past tense oder *past perfect tense?*

example: Jack (go) home after he (eat) his sandwich. →
Jack went home after he had eaten his sandwich.

1. The man (tell) me that he (not see) me before.
2. They (ask) me what books I (read).
3. I (hear) that the baby (start) to cry in the bedroom.
4. They (have) ice-cream after they (finish) dinner.
5. Alexandra (tell) the teacher that she (find) the word in the dictionary.
6. Leo (must) do all the work he (forget) to do the day before.
7. Mr Smith (go) out after his wife (come) home.
8. The woman (take) the coat after she (pay) £ 100.

16

Wie bei *exercise* 15, nur etwas schwieriger.

1. We (like) Greek food as soon as we (taste) it.
2. After Robin (arrive) we (start) playing tennis.
3. I (ask) James why he (not visit) us before.
4. The lights (go) out before I (be) ready to go.
5. Billy (drink) some beer after his dad (tell) him not to do so.
6. Romy (smoke) her first cigarette before she (be) fourteen.
7. Clarissa (learn) English before she (come) to America.
8. After our plane (land), we (have) to wait for our luggage.

2

Es geht so weiter wie bei den zwei vorhergehenden *exercises.* Setze die Zeitwörter in der Klammer in die richtige Zeitstufe. Dieses Mal gibt es auch Punkte dafür!

❍❍ 1. The sun (shine) yesterday after it (be) cold for many weeks.
❍❍ 2. Uncle David (go) to the doctor after he (be) ill for a month.
❍❍ 3. Before the police (catch) the thief, he (steal) two more watches.
❍❍ 4. Mum once (paint) a picture although she (never, learn) it.
❍❍ 5. I (not tell) my teacher that my mum (help) me with my homework.
❍❍❍ 6. I (be) very angry when I (see) that my brother (eat) my apple.
❍❍ 7. The bike (be) much more expensive than he (think) at first.
❍❍ 8. Dad (drive) me home after I (fall) into the water.
❍❍ 9. Marion (ask) me what (happen) to me last week.
❍❍ 10. We (eat) two Big Macs before we (go) home.
❍❍ 11. Paul (not say) that he (take) Albert's watch.
❍❍ 12. The days (become) colder after it (snow).
❍❍ 13. Martin (tell) me that he (be) to London.
❍❍ 14. I (feel) great after I (pass) the exam.
❍❍ 15. It (be) Fred who (clean) the room.
❍❍❍ 16. When I (get) off the bike I (see) that one of the tires (lose) air.

Alles über 31 Punkte verdient **großes Lob**! Wenn du weniger Punkte hast: Stelle fest, woran es liegt!
Hast du das (falsche) Zeitwort in die (falsche) Zeitstufe gesetzt? Dann liegt ein Denkproblem vor.
Kannst du die Zeitstufen nicht richtig bilden? Dann hast du ein Lernproblem!

ERDKNÖPFE UND RAUMKNÖPFE

Du liest etwas, kannst es dir aber nur schwer merken?

Halte deine Erdknöpfe:

Du berührst mit je zwei Fingern der einen Hand den Rand deines Schambeins und mit zwei Fingern der anderen Hand den Punkt unterhalb der Unterlippe.

Dauer der Übung: 2 Minuten

Passieren dir Fehler beim Abschreiben von der Tafel?

Halte deine Raumknöpfe:

Du berührst mit zwei Fingern der einen Hand das Steißbein. Es befindet sich am unteren Ende der Wirbelsäule. Mit zwei Fingern der anderen Hand berührst du den Punkt oberhalb der Oberlippe.
Die Erdknöpfe und Raumknöpfe kannst du auch sanft massieren.

Dauer der Übung: 2 Minuten

Die Leideform

☆ ***Passive voice*** drückt aus, dass **mit dem Subjekt etwas geschieht,** es „erleidet" etwas.

Du bildest *passive voice* mit
to be + past participle (3rd form).

*Parliament **is opened** by the Queen every year.*
(Mit dem Parlament geschieht etwas; es wird eröffnet.)

☆ Das Gegenstück zu *passive voice* ist ***active voice,*** die Tätigkeitsform. Hier ist das Subjekt selbst aktiv, das heißt, es tut etwas.

Jede **passive Handlung** (bei der mit dem Subjekt etwas geschieht) kann **auch in der Tätigkeitsform *(active voice)* dargestellt** werden.

*The Queen **opens** the Parliament every year.*
(Eine aktive Queen also, die etwas tut.)

active to passive

A large crowd (= Menge)	*welcomed*	*the Queen.*
The Queen	*was welcomed*	*by a large crowd.*

1 Das Subjekt deines (neuen) passiven Satzes ist das Objekt des aktiven Satzes (das ist der Ausgangssatz); du brauchst ja schließlich etwas am Beginn des Satzes!

2 Das Prädikat (Zeitwort) wird passiv, das heißt, es teilt sich auf in die passende Form von *to be* und das *past participle* (dritte Grundform). **Achtung:** In der gleichen Zeitstufe bleiben!

3 Manchmal wird das Subjekt des aktiven Satzes zum Objekt das passiven Satzes (das sogenannte ***by-object***). Das ist dann sinnvoll, wenn du den Verursacher der Handlung *(agent)* angeben willst.

passive to active

1 Das Objekt des passiven Satzes wird zum Subjekt des aktiven Satzes. Wenn dein passiver Satz kein *by-object* enthält, musst du dir eines suchen. Du nimmst am besten ein ganz neutrales, wie z. B. *by them* oder *by somebody.*

2 Das passive Prädikat (Zeitwortgruppe) wird zum aktiven Prädikat. Es verliert dabei die Form von *to be,* und das Hauptzeitwort passt sich an (in Person, Zahl, Zeit).

3 Das passive Subjekt wird zum aktiven Objekt.

The doors	*were closed*	*(by them)*	*at ten o'clock.*
They	*closed*	*the doors*	*at ten o'clock.*

17

Du musst die passenden Zeiten erkennen und die angegebenen Zeitwörter mit ihrer richtigen passiven Form einsetzen *(form of to be + past participle)*. Jeder Satz enthält einen eindeutigen Hinweis auf die richtige Zeitstufe. (Du hast es übrigens nur mit *present tense* und *past tense* zu tun.)

example: Luckily nobody (kill) in last night's accident. →
Luckily nobody was killed in last night's accident.
(Der eindeutige Hinweis auf *past tense* ist *"last night"*.)

1. All these postcards (send) to us by our friends last week.
2. Every year a thousand new one-family homes (build) in this state.
3. In 1905 the first Model-T car (produce) by the Ford Motor Company.
4. The new casino (visit) by more than 2,000 people every day.
5. "Nessie", the monster of Loch Ness, (see) by tourists every summer.
6. The 1994 Football World Cup (win) by Brazil.
7. The really good computer games (usually, install) on the C: drive.
8. Why are the walls in your classroom so dirty? They (paint) only last year. (= erst im letzten Jahr)

18

Bilde alle Fragen und die Verneinung zu den folgenden Sätzen.

example: The Queen was welcomed at the airport by a large crowd. →
Was the Queen welcomed at the airport by a large crowd?
Who was welcomed at the airport by a large crowd?
Where was the Queen welcomed by a large crowd?
By whom was the Queen welcomed at the airport?
The Queen was not welcomed at the airport by a large crowd.

1. St. Paul's Cathedral was built by Sir Christopher Wren in the seventeenth century.
2. These books were written by a young girl during the war.
3. The New Year's Concert is heard by millions of people in more than eighty countries every year.

19

Du musst umwandeln, und zwar *active to passive* (die ersten vier Sätze) und *passive to active*. Achte darauf, dass die Zeitstufen erhalten bleiben!

examples: Mozart wrote "The Magic Flute". →
"The Magic Flute" **was written** by Mozart.

Our bags were checked by a friendly policeman. →
A friendly policeman **checked** our bags.

1. Millions of people saw "Titanic" in 1998.
2. They sent the documents to the wrong address.
3. This restaurant serves excellent food.
4. They make very good cars in Japan.
5. Millions of Schillings are spent by tourists in our country every year.
6. English is spoken in most parts of the world.
7. Two men were arrested after the robbery.
8. "Faust" was not written by Schiller.

In dieser Schulstufe kommen neue Zeitstufen dazu:

future tense:	***will be + past participle***
present perfect tense:	***have/has been + past participle***
past perfect tense:	***had been + past participle***

R

Die Bildung der *passive voice* in diesen drei Zeilen ist recht einfach. Du gehst nach dem bekannten Rezept vor:

form of "to be" + past participle

20 Setze die folgenden passiven Sätze in *future tense* (Sätze 1–3), *present perfect tense* (4, 5) und *past perfect tense* (6–8).

examples: "Stargate" (show) at our cinema until the end of the month. →
"Stargate" will be shown at our cinema until the end of . . .

The doors (close). You can't get in. →
The doors have been closed. You can't get in.

After the President (welcome), the concert began. →
After the President had been welcomed, the concert began.

1. The boxes (send) to your house next week.
2. Hundreds of guests (invite) to the opening of the new theatre next year.
3. The next Olympic games (hold) in the USA in the year 2000.
4. The drinks (serve), now the party can begin.
5. This programme (bring) to you by the Coca-Cola Company!
6. Everybody went to bed after the lights (switch) off.
7. After the doors (shut), nobody could get in.
8. The pyramids of Mexico (finish) long before Cortez and his men arrived.

21 *Active to passive,* dieses Mal mit *future tense* und *present perfect tense* (in Dreierblöcken). Achte darauf, dass die angegebenen Zeiten erhalten bleiben!

1. They will open the new motorway next Saturday.
2. Stephen Spielberg will direct "Batman IV" next year.
3. They will stop the match if the rain gets worse.
4. They have cut down the oldest trees in our street.
5. People have put little flags in every window. It looks lovely.
6. Walt Disney Studios have made "Jungle Book" into a very funny film.

In der **indirekten Rede** *(reported speech* oder *indirect speech)* wird unter bestimmten Umständen ***past perfect tense*** verwendet. Sie entsteht aus *past tense* oder *present perfect tense.* (Mehr davon ab Seite 78.)

direct speech:	*Dad said, "My jeans*	***have*** *not been washed."*
reported speech:	*Dad said (that) his jeans*	***had*** *not been washed.*

direct speech:	*Maggie said, "My CD-player*	***was*** *made in Japan."*
reported speech:	*Maggie said (that) her CD-player*	***had been*** *made in Japan.*

22

Bilde Sätze in *reported speech.* Verwende dabei *past perfect tense, passive voice.*

1. The policeman said, "Three bikes and a car were stolen on Monday."
2. Eve said, "The date of my birthday party has been changed."
3. Susie said, "I was invited to dinner at Charlie's place."
4. Our neighbours said, "Our house was built in 1968."
5. Paul told us, "We were woken up by a loud noise."
6. The waiter said, "Dinner has been served, sir."
7. Bill said, "My car has been repaired."
8. Maywell shouted, "I have been bitten by a dog!"

1

Bilde passive Sätze aus den folgenden Angaben. Achte dabei besonders auf die richtigen Zeiten. (Es kommen *present tense, past tense, future tense, present perfect tense* und *past perfect tense* vor.)

❍ 1. Jackie's leg (hurt) in a skiing accident last winter.
❍ 2. In the old days the Tower of London (use) as a prison.
❍ 3. Oh, look! Two of my nicest cups (break)!
❍ 4. What a terrible film! I'm sure it (forget) in a few years' time.
❍ 5. English is the Number One language. It (speak) all over the world.
❍ 6. We checked that all doors (close) before we went to bed.
❍ 7. Look! The old apple tree in our garden (blow) over by the storm.
❍ 8. The picture (finish) next week.
❍ 9. We (invite) to Mario's birthday party. Shall we go?
❍ 10. Our car is at the garage. It (take) there yesterday.

Wenn du 9 oder 10 richtige Sätze geschafft hast, bist du ***active Passive-champ!***

PAUSE

Frage und Verneinung

Alle passiven Sätze enthalten Hilfszeitwörter *(the forms of to be, have, has, will, . . .)*, mit denen du direkt – das heißt **ohne Umschreibung** mit *do, does, did* – fragen und verneinen kannst. Frage und Verneinung stehen in derselben Zeitstufe wie der Ausgangssatz.

23

Ask all questions and negate! Aber bitte nicht alle Sätze auf einmal!

1. The factory will be shut down because it is not modern enough.
2. The Matterhorn is climbed by hundreds of tourists every year.
3. Breakfast will be served downstairs from 8 to 9:30.
4. Gold was found here 100 years ago.
5. The walls of the house have been painted.
6. The tigers were fed this morning.

Sätze mit zwei Objekten

Wenn du aus einem aktiven Satz einen passiven machen willst, brauchst du unbedingt ein **Objekt**:

active: *They have not opened* ***this door*** *for a hundred years.*
passive: ***This door*** *has not been opened for a hundred years.*

Es gibt aber – im Englischen genauso wie im Deutschen – **Sätze mit zwei Objekten**, einem „Personalobjekt" und einem „Sachobjekt":

Aunt Julia	*sent*	***my brother***	***a telegram.***
Grandfather	*gave*	***me***	***some money.***

Bei Sätzen mit **zwei Objekten** lassen sich auch **zwei Passivsätze** bilden:

1. *A telegram was sent **to** my brother by Aunt Julia.*
2. *My brother was sent a telegram by Aunt Julia.*

1. *Some money was given **to** me by grandfather.*
2. *I was given some money by grandfather.*

1. *The new room was shown **to** us by Gloria.*
2. *We were shown the new room by Gloria.*

Das **„Personalobjekt"** *(my brother, me, us)* wird im Englischen **viel häufiger** zur Bildung eines passiven Satzes herangezogen als das „Sachobjekt" *(a telegram, some money, the new room).* Man nennt diese Form dann auch *personal passive*.

Wenn das „Personalobjekt" ein ***personal pronoun*** (persönliches Fürwort) ist – also etwa *me, her, him, us, them* –, steht es als Subjekt des passiven Satzes natürlich im 1. Fall *(subject case).*

*They offered **me** a good job.*
***I** was offered a good job.*

*They offered **him** . . .*
***He** was offered . . .*

*They offered **us** . . .*
***We** were offered . . .*

*They offered **her** . . .*
***She** was offered . . .*

*They offered **them** . . .*
***They** were offered . . .*

Im Deutschen ist diese Form des Passivs nicht immer möglich. Wir greifen in solchen Fällen gerne zu den so genannten **„man"-Sätzen**:

Man hat ihm ein Telegramm geschickt.
Man hat mir etwas Geld gegeben.
Man bot ihm einen guten Job an.

24 An die Arbeit, *ladies and gentlemen*! Bildet passive Sätze mit dem *personal object*.

1. They gave my sister a better room in the youth hostel.
2. Somebody will show you the computer room.
3. They have paid the mechanic for his work.
4. They called him the "Red Baron".
5. They will tell you to come back next week.
6. They have offered my dad a bigger car.
7. Somebody promised him a lot of money.
8. They taught us how to eat with chopsticks (= Essstäbchen).

the passive progressive

Passive voice ist auch bei Sätzen möglich, in denen *progressive form* vorkommt. Das sieht dann so aus:

They are painting the garage door. →
The garage door ***is being painted.***

They were closing the shop when we arrived. →
The shop ***was being closed*** *when we arrived.*

R ***Passive progressive*** ist nur in ***present tense*** und ***past tense*** üblich. Und so wird *passive progressive* gebildet:

25 Bilde passive Sätze mit *progressive form* unter dem Motto: „Was geht hier gerade vor?"

example: We can't visit the castle. They are still restoring it. →
We can't visit the castle. It is still being restored.
(to restore = restaurieren)

1. You can't go in. They are decorating the Christmas tree.
2. When I woke up they were cleaning my rooms.
3. When I looked out of the window I saw that they were towing away my car. (to tow away = abschleppen)
4. They were still playing loud music when we left the party.
5. They were cooking breakfast while it was still dark.
6. Where's Sean? – Inside. They are showing him around the house.
7. I have to walk to work today because they are still repairing my car.
8. They were still repairing the tables when the guests arrived.
9. They are developing the films today, so I'll show you the pictures tomorrow. (to develop = entwickeln)
10. Ford and Mercedes are testing the new brake system. (brake = Bremse)
11. The city is building two hundred new apartments for young couples.
12. They were still checking the sound system when the Rolling Stones came onto the stage.

Benny: "My aunt is having a new Baby."
Lenny: "Why? What was wrong with the old one?"

the passive infinitive

*You **can see** the sea from here.*	→	*The sea **can be seen** from here.*
*We **cannot open** this door.*	→	*This door **cannot be opened.***
*You **must study** these articles.*	→	*These articles **must be studied.***
*We **need not** read this story.*	→	*This story **need not be read.***
*You **should inform** someone.*	→	*Someone **should be informed.***

Hilfszeitwort + *to be* + *past participle*

Eigentlich „funktioniert" *passive infinitive* nach demselben Prinzip wie alle anderen Passivformen. Einziger Unterschied: das Hilfszeitwort!

26

Bilde Sätze mit *passive infinitive.* Beachte dabei, dass du das Hilfszeitwort des aktiven Satzes weiterverwenden musst.

1. Visitors may feed the animals from 8 to 9 o'clock.
2. They could not answer the questions.
3. We have to wash the car today.
4. They must not sell alcohol to young people.
5. You need not do this exercise today.
6. You should answer the letter before Friday.
7. They will use the energy of the sun some day.
8. You should not touch wild animals.
9. You can post letters and packages from 7 a.m. to 7 p.m.
10. You must print all the answers on the question sheet.
    (to print = in Druckschrift schreiben)
11. You can visit lots of interesting museums in London.
12. They had to take the old man to hospital.

Hilfszeitwörter der Aussageweise

modal verbs in verschiedenen Zeitstufen

present tense:	*Tom*	***can*** ***may*** ***must***	*play tennis.*
past tense:	*Tom*	***could / was able to*** ***was allowed to*** ***had to***	*play tennis.*
future tense:	*Tom*	***will be able to*** ***will be allowed to*** ***will have to***	*play tennis.*
present perfect:	*Tom*	***has been able to*** ***has been allowed to*** ***has had to***	*play tennis.*
past perfect:	*Tom*	***had been able to*** ***had been allowed to*** ***had had to***	*play tennis.*
conditional present:	*Tom*	***would be able to*** ***would be allowed to*** ***would have to***	*play tennis.*
conditional perfect:	*Tom*	***would have been able to*** ***would have been allowed to*** ***would have had to***	*play . . .*

Sieh dir die folgenden Beispiele an. Sie sollen dir helfen, „können, dürfen und müssen" in den verschiedenen Zeiten auszudrücken.

☆ *George* ***(may) watch*** *the western on TV last night.*

Klar, dass *last night past tense* verlangt. →
George was allowed to watch *the western on TV last night.*

☆ *My mum* ***(can) speak*** *German since she was a little child.*

Klar, dass *since she was a little child present perfect* verlangt. →
My mum has been able to speak *German since she was a little girl.*

☆ *You* ***(must) go*** *to football practice tomorrow.*

Klar, dass *tomorrow future tense* verlangt. →
You will have to go *to football practice tomorrow.*

☆ *We* ***(can) see*** *the mountains from here if the weather were better.*

Klar, dass *if the weather were better conditional present* verlangt. →
We would be able to see *the mountains from here if the weather . . .*

27 Setze die folgenden Sätze in die richtige Zeitstufe. Du kannst sie an bestimmten Hinweisen im Satz eindeutig erkennen; einmal ist die gesuchte Zeitstufe auch angegeben.

1. Adam (must) milk the cows every morning.
2. If we (can) help you, we would do it, of course.
3. Our car doesn't work. Dad (must) take it to the mechanic tomorrow.
4. You (may) go to the concert if you had asked your parents.
5. Bill and I enjoyed the horrorfilm on TV last night, but my little brother (may, not) watch it.
6. I hope I (can) play again next Sunday. I feel better already.
7. Mum is tired and she is going to bed. She (must) wash and iron our clothes all day. *(present perfect)*
8. We (can) understand them if we spoke their language.

1

Setze die richtigen Formen und Zeiten der *modal verbs* ein.

example: Last year on New Year's Eve we . . . stay up until three o'clock in the morning. (dürfen) →
Last year on New Year's Eve we were allowed to stay up until three o'clock in the morning.

If you had asked me earlier, I . . . help you. (können) →
If you had asked me earlier, I would have been able to help you.

❍ 1. Dad ____________________ take the train to work last week because his car did not work. (müssen)

❍ 2. If I lived in Austria or Switzerland, I ____________________ ski perfectly. (können)

❍ 3. You mustn't drive a car now, Willie, because you are too young. But you ____________________ drive when you are eighteen. (dürfen)

❍ 4. Jackie ____________________ play the guitar since his seventh birthday. (können)

❍❍❍ 5. ____________________ you come to my place today? We ____________________ play table tennis or we ____________________ watch a video film. (können, 3x)

❍ 6. If you don't take a shower today, you ____________________ take one tomorrow. (müssen)

❍ 7. Charlie ____________________ ride a bike since he was three years old. (können)

❍ 8. If I help my mother in the house all week, I (may) ____________ go to the cinema on Saturday. (dürfen)

Alle 10 richtig? ***Fantastic!*** Wenn nicht, wiederhole noch einmal die Seiten 45 und 46.

GEHIRNKNÖPFE

Schon ein wenig müde vom letzten Kapitel?

Da wollen wir mal deine Gehirntätigkeit wieder auf Vordermann bringen. Man könnte auch aktivieren dazu sagen: Du berührst mit zwei Fingern der linken Hand den Nabel. Den Daumen der anderen Hand legst du in das rechte Grübchen unterhalb deines Schlüsselbeins. Mit Zeige- und Mittelfinger berührst du das linke Grübchen. Nun massierst du mit leichtem Druck alle drei Stellen gleichzeitig. Nach etwa einer Minute wechselst du die Hände. Nun reiben die Finger der rechten Hand den Nabel, die linke Hand befindet sich beim Schlüsselbein.

Dauer der Übung: 2 Minuten

Frage und Verneinung

In den letzten zwei Jahren hast du dich ausführlich mit der Bildung von Frage und Verneinung beschäftigt. Wenn du nicht mehr so genau weißt, wie das grundsätzlich geht, schau in den ersten zwei Bänden von „Durchstarten in Englisch" nach! Dort wird dir alles einfach und übersichtlich erklärt!

Aber – der Mensch lernt nicht aus! Es gibt noch immer einige Dinge über *questions and negation* zu berichten und zu lernen! Und zwar:

- ☆ Fragen nach dem Objekt (Ergänzung)
- ☆ Fragen in allen Zeitstufen
- ☆ die negative Frage in längeren Sätzen
- ☆ die negative *why*-Frage
- ☆ Fragen nach Beifügungen

Normalerweise kommen diese fünf Punkte nicht einzeln und getrennt vor, sondern gleichzeitig und durcheinander gemischt!

Aber keine Angst! Das alles ist nicht besonders schwierig, denn im Grunde genommen musst du nur immer wieder das anwenden, was du schon gelernt hast. Das heißt, du lernst jetzt nichts absolut Neues mehr, sondern du vertiefst nur mehr das, was du schon kennst.

28 Fangen wir am besten mit einer Wiederholungsübung an. Stelle Fragen mit den in Klammer stehenden Fragewörtern und bilde einen negativen (verneinten) Satz:

example: Our friends wanted to bring us Easter eggs in the morning. (who, who(m), what, when) →

Who wanted to bring us Easter eggs in the morning?

What did our friends want to bring us in the morning?

Who(m) did our friends want to bring Easter eggs in the morning?

When did our friends want to bring us Easter eggs?

Our friends did not want to bring us Easter eggs in the morning.

1. Nick wrote two letters last night. (who, what, when)

Mit dem Lösungsheft überprüfen! Erst wenn alles richtig ist, weitermachen!

2. We found the bike behind the house. (what, where)
3. Terry had ten marbles in her pocket. (who, how many, where)

Genug für heute! Morgen weiterüben!

4. In the evening the men played chess (= Schach). (who, what, when)
5. They gave me twenty Schillings for doing the washing up. (who(m), what, how much)
6. Mr Kinnock taught me English four years ago. (what, who(m), when)

Alles richtig? Morgen gibt's den Rest!

7. Snoopy was playing in the garden during the rain. (where, when)
8. Max drank a lot of wine yesterday evening. (what, when)
9. I bought two pounds of potatoes at the grocer's this morning. (who, what, where)
10. We got the worst seats because we were late. (what, why)

Gehe erst zum nächsten Abschnitt weiter, wenn du acht von zehn Beispielen richtig gelöst hast.

Fragen nach dem Objekt

☆ ***what*** oder ***who(m)***?

Jacob likes ***English*** *best.*
What *does Jacob like best?*
Mum bought ***this dress*** *in Rome.*
What *did mum buy in Rome?*
Dad always brings ***mum*** *flowers.*
Who(m) *does dad always bring flowers?*
John told ***us*** *an interesting story.*
Who(m) *did John tell an interesting story?*

Schon erkannt, wie die Sache funktioniert?

! ***what*** für Dinge – ***who*** für Personen

29 Frage nach den Objekten der folgenden Sätze: *who or what?*

1. I asked the boys to help me with the tree house.
2. They gave her a T-shirt, too.
3. My parents want to sell our car.
4. Mrs Curtis told the children to be quiet.
5. Jackie got a reggae-CD from her friends.
6. Grandma sent me a nice birthday present.
7. Joseph often rides his new bike in the afternoon.
8. Mary found a golden ring in a telephone box.
9. They have finished the new shopping centre after six years.
10. Aunt Liz showed the girls the little kittens. (kittens = Kätzchen)
11. Mum's boss offered her a better job.
12. Dad will take us to "Disney World" next summer.

☆ ***whom*** oder ***who***?

TIPP

Beides ist möglich! Und beides hat Vorteile.

- Wenn du ***whom*** verwendest, vermeidest du jede Verwechslung mit der Frage nach dem Subjekt.
- Wenn du ***who*** verwendest, sprichst oder schreibst du modernes Alltagsenglisch.

Die Entscheidung liegt bei dir. Die „bessere" Wahl ist aber *who;* sie wird auch von *"native speakers"* bevorzugt!

☆ Frage nach **zwei Objekten**

Uncle Bill gave me some football stickers.

me	*some football stickers*
↓	↓
Personalobjekt	Sachobjekt
who(m)?	*what?*

Who(m) did Uncle Bill give some football stickers?
What did Uncle Bill give me?

Achte besonders auf Sätze wie diesen (Kombination verb + preposition):

Jenny waits for me at the bus stop every morning.

Hier kannst du auf mehrere Arten nach dem Objekt fragen. Eine davon ist „besser" als die anderen (→ →).

For whom *does Jenny wait at the bus stop every morning?*
Whom *does Jenny wait* ***for*** *at the bus stop every morning?*
→ → ***Who*** *does Jenny wait* ***for*** *at the bus stop every morning?*

This book is about Napoleon.
→ → ***Who*** *is this book* ***about****?*

Ronny is looking for a cheap mountain bike.
→ → ***What*** *is Ronny looking* ***for****?*

Bilde die „beste" Objektfrage (→ →).

1. Yesterday Willie <u>spoke with</u> Mary.
2. You are <u>looking at</u> my favourite sister.
3. We often <u>think of</u> our holidays in Arizona.
4. Michael is <u>thinking of</u> Sarah.
5. My parents <u>talked about</u> our neigbours last night.
6. This morning the bus <u>waited for</u> me.
7. Grandpa often <u>plays with</u> my little brother.
8. Mum is <u>looking for</u> Sally. (to look for = suchen)
9. My family and I usually <u>listen to</u> BBC.
10. Most people <u>hope for</u> a "white Christmas".

Fragen in allen Zeitstufen

☆ ***present simple*** und ***past simple*** werden **ohne Hilfszeitwörter** gebildet:

Daraus folgt, dass bei diesen beiden Zeitstufen die Fragen mit ***do / does*** oder mit ***did*** gebildet werden (mit Ausnahme der Subjektfrage natürlich).

present tense:	***do***	*.......... I, you, we, they*
	does	*...... he, she, it*
past tense:	***did***	*......... (all persons)*

☆ **Alle anderen Zeitstufen** werden **mit Hilfszeitwörtern** gebildet. Daher werden Frage und Verneinung **nicht mit *do, does*** oder ***did*** gebildet, sondern mit Hilfe der Umstellung von Subjekt und Hilfszeitwort.

Wenn man von dir also verlangt, zu irgendeinem Satz Frage und Verneinung zu bilden, solltest du so vorgehen:

1. Überprüfe, ob das Prädikat ein Hilfszeitwort enthält oder nicht.
2. Wenn ja, verwende es bei Frage und Verneinung weiter.
3. Wenn nein, umschreibe es mit *do, does* oder *did.*

Zur Veranschaulichung einige Beispiele:

future: Princess Anne ***will*** *open* the new hospital in a few weeks.

↓ ↓

Hilfszeitwort Hauptzeitwort

Will Princess Anne *open* the new hospital in a few weeks?
Who **will** *open* the new hospital in a few weeks?
What **will** Princess Anne *open* in a few weeks?
When **will** Princess Anne *open* the new hospital?
Princess Anne ***will*** **not** *open* the new hospital in a few weeks.

present perfect: Tony ***has*** *worn* his Dr Martens since last Sunday.

Has Tony *worn* his Dr Martens since last Sunday?
Who **has** *worn* his Dr Martens since last Sunday?
What **has** Tony *worn* since last Sunday?
Since when **has** Tony *worn* his Dr Martens?
Tony **has not** *worn* his Dr Martens since last Sunday.

past perfect: Tracy ***had*** *talked* to her teacher before she left school.

Had Tracy *talked* to her teacher before she left school?
Who **had** *talked* to her teacher before she left school?
Who(m) **had** Tracy *talked* to before she left school?
When **had** Tracy *talked* to her teacher?
Tracy **had not** *talked* to her teacher before she left school.

conditional present: Bill ***would*** *help* us tomorrow if he could.

Would Bill *help* us tomorrow if he could?
Who ***would*** *help* us tomorrow if he could?
Who ***would*** Bill *help* tomorrow if he could?
When ***would*** Bill *help* us if he could?
Bill ***would not*** *help* us if he could.

conditional perfect: Bill ***would*** *have helped* us if we had asked him.

Would Bill *have helped* us if we had asked him?
Who ***would*** *have helped* us if we had asked (him)?
Who ***would*** Bill *have helped* if we had asked him?
Bill ***would not*** *help* us if we had asked him.

Das gleiche gilt auch für die ***progressive form***. Sie wird auch mit einem Hilfszeitwort – in diesem Fall von ***to be*** – gebildet:

Are you *taking* a shower?
Am I *speaking* with Mr James Brown?
Is the water *boiling*?
What ***were*** you *doing* when I called you last night?
When ***will*** you ***be*** *talking* to Ms Middleton again?
Was it *raining* when you left your house this morning?
Since when ***has*** that tree ***been*** *standing* there?
How long ***have*** you ***been*** *waiting* for us?

31 Bilde Fragen und Verneinung in den jeweils angegebenen Zeitstufen. Bei der Frage nach dem Objekt ist die „beste“ Möglichkeit gefragt!

example: Charlie has been waiting for Susi at the bus-stop since 10.
(who, who . . . for, where, since when) →
Who has been waiting for Susi at the bus-stop since 10?
Who has Charlie been waiting for at the bus-stop since 10?
Where has Charlie been waiting for Susi since 10?
Since when has Charlie been waiting for Susi?

1. Henry has given me the key to his house. (who, who(m), what)

Schau gleich im Lösungsheft nach, ob deine Antworten stimmen!

2. We are going to see Jim tomorrow. (who, who(m), when)
3. Our neighbour sold his dog because it was so wild. (what, why)

Morgen weitermachen!

4. They arrived at six o’clock because it was raining. (when, why)
5. We have been waiting for you for hours. (who, who(m) . . . , how long)
6. They liked Carina very much. (who(m), how)

Wenn alles stimmt, kommt morgen der Rest dran!

7. The Professor spoke quietly all evening. (how, how long)
8. Jane went home quickly after the concert. (who, how, when)

Merke dir unbedingt:

Negative Fragen in längeren Sätzen

„Negative Frage" heißt: „**Warum** ist etwas **nicht** geschehen?" oder „**Warum** ist jemand **nicht** hier?" Die Grundlagen dazu hast du bereits erarbeitet. (Siehe dazu auch „Durchstarten in Englisch für die 6. Schulstufe", Seite 63.)

Aber es ist ein Unterschied, ob man das mit kurzen Sätzen macht oder ob man sich mit langen englischen Ausführungen herumschlagen muss!

32

Zur Erinnerung und Auffrischung: Du musst mit der Verneinung des Verbs oder Hilfszeitwortes beginnen. Bilde also negative Fragen nach dem folgenden Muster, aber mache nicht alle Beispiele auf einmal! „Mach mal Pause!"

example: Alexandra is in the park with the girls. →
Isn't Alexandra in the park with the girls?

Marcel lives in Paris now. →
Doesn't Marcel live in Paris now?

1. A good farmer feeds his animals early in the morning.
2. You were riding Kevin's new bike all day yesterday.
3. Nancy has written three letters since this morning.
4. Sue has told us not to smoke inside the house.
5. Henry began to study for his maths test today.
6. Tom will be waiting for us outside the school.
7. They will climb the hill when it stops raining.
8. The British queue up at every bus stop.
9. You have seen me in the park before.
10. They wanted to go home earlier.
11. The river freezes in winter.
12. Mary can play the piano very nicely.

negative *why*-Fragen

Je mehr du Englisch lernst und je mehr du englische Texte liest – immer wieder wirst du auf diese Art der Frage stoßen. Man fragt nämlich recht oft danach, **warum jemand etwas nicht tut oder getan hat.**

Das sieht dann so aus:

Judy didn't go home, because she had a lot of money with her.
Why didn't Judy go *home? – Because she had a lot . . .*

Sandra hasn't called us for over a week.
Why hasn't Sandra called us *for over a week?*

Molly doesn't want to see me any more.
Why doesn't Molly want *to see you (me) any more?*

33

Bilde negative *why*-Fragen mit den folgenden Beispielen.

1. William didn't tell us the story because it was a secret.
2. Aunt Sally won't ride her bike again because she thinks she is too old.
3. Dad can't play the violin any more because he has hurt his hand.
4. They haven't waited for me because it is too cold.
5. They didn't close the door softly because they were in a hurry.
6. Frank didn't hide it in his pocket.
7. George didn't ride the big black horse.
8. Sonya doesn't want to walk home at night.
9. You didn't sleep well in the tent. (tent = Zelt)
10. Betty didn't say anything when she left the room.
11. He won't leave the house as long as Freddy is sleeping.
12. You didn't bring me another glass of beer.

Fragen nach Beifügungen

*Mr Wilson played only a **small** part in the new TV-show.*

***Which** part did Mr Wilson play in the new TV-show?*
(Welche Rolle spielte . . . ?)

(What kind of part did Mr Wilson play in the new TV-show?)
(Welche Art von Rolle spielte . . . ?)

In diesem Mustersatz ist ***small*** die Beifügung zu ***part***.

34 Frage nach den jeweiligen Beifügungen. Achte besonders auf die gegebenen Zeiten und Zeitwortformen, denn danach richten sich deine Fragen!

1. "Lenny" is the smartest dog in the world.
2. The youngest boy knew the answer.
3. Sam wanted to buy the red roses.
4. Robin bought the cheapest car.
5. The old man showed us the shortest way.
6. Mum has always liked sweet red wine best.
7. The boys could not answer the difficult questions.
8. Dennis was a very clever student.
9. I don't like violent films. (violent = gewalttätig, brutal)
10. Jamie spoke in a very low voice.
11. They wanted to win the international championship.
12. I would like to have the fastest computer in my class.

1

Hier triffst du auf eine Auswahl verschiedenster Sätze. Deine Aufgabe ist es nun, verschiedene Arten von Fragen zu stellen oder die Sätze zu verneinen – wie du es in diesem Kapitel wiederholt oder gelernt hast. Frage also nach den unterstrichenen Satzteilen oder bilde Fragen mit den angegebenen Fragewörtern.

❍❍ 1. Maggie will call you next week.
❍ 2. I have asked Tobias for help, but not Simon. (negative "why"?)
❍❍❍❍ 3. Harry gave me some sweets because he likes me.
❍❍❍ 4. We wanted to go to Italy last summer. (negative question)
❍❍ 5. Derek hast just spoken with his boss.
❍ 6. My dad has built a wonderful garden grill.
❍❍❍ 7. We have been working since 7 o'clock. (negative question)
❍❍❍ 8. Cindy must look after the baby because her mum and dad are going out tonight. (negation)
❍❍ 9. Tom did not wait for the late night film because he was tired.
❍ 10. The oldest wolf leads the pack. (pack = Rudel)
❍❍ 11. Ferry and Joe haven't come to the party. (negative "why"?)
❍ 12. We talked about Rita's boyfriend for a long time.
❍❍❍ 13. Marlon did not wait for us after school. (negative question)

Wie viele von den 28 Punkten hast du erreicht? Alle? Dann bist du – *without question* – **der Größte und Beste**!
27 bis 25? Du bist noch immer **groß**, kannst aber noch wachsen.
24 bis 20? **Mittelgroßklein**.
Weniger als 20? Du näherst dich dem **Zwergenstadium**! Wenn du fragemäßig wachsen willst, musst du ohne weitere Frage noch fleißig üben. Noch irgendwelche Fragen?

Die Zeitstufen – eine Übersicht

Die folgende Tabelle mit allen Zeitstufen der englischen Sprache soll dir einen Überblick bieten. Du hast noch nicht alle Zeitstufen gelernt und kannst vielleicht mit einigen Begriffen, die du hier vorfindest, nicht viel anfangen. Lass dich aber nicht verwirren! Sieh nur dort nach, wo du möchtest, und betrachte die „unbekannten" Dinge als besondere Serviceleistung! Du wirst sie in den nächsten Jahren sicher irgendwann einmal brauchen können.

Damit die Sache übersichtlicher und klarer wird, verwenden wir ein sehr bekanntes Wort: ***"to write"***.

tense	**active voice**	
	simple form	**progressive form**
present	write, writes	am, is, are writing
past	wrote	was, were writing
future (will)	will (shall) write	will (shall) be writing
present perfect	have, has written	have, has been writing
past perfect	had written	had been writing
future perfect	will (. . .) have written	will (. . .) have been writing
conditional pres.	would write	would be writing
conditional perf.	would have written	would have been writing

tense	passive voice	
	simple form	progressive form
present	am, is, are written	am, is, are being written
past	was, were written	was, were being written
future (will)	will (shall) be written	—
present perfect	have, has been written	—
past perfect	had been written	—
future perfect	will (. . .) have been written	—
conditional pres.	would be written	—
conditional perf.	would have been written	—

Can you find out what tenses are hidden in these jokes?

Patient: "You've got to help me, Doctor. I think I'm a ghost."
Doctor: "I had the feeling that was your problem when I saw you walk through the wall."

Mother: "Billy, you mustn't fight! I've told you again and again, you should learn to give and take."
Billy: "I did. I gave Tommy a black eye and took his apple."

Kinder, wie die Zeit vergeht - Übungen zu den bekannten Zeiten

In der Zeitentabelle auf den vorhergehenden zwei Seiten hast du (hoffentlich!) alle Zeiten erkannt, die du schon gelernt hast. Damit du sie nicht so schnell vergisst und nicht aus der Übung kommst, bieten wir dir auf den folgenden Seiten die Gelegenheit, diese Zeiten zu üben und zu üben und zu üben und . . .

Vergiss aber nicht: Nach jedem Übungsblock unbedingt eine Pause einlegen!

35 Bei dieser Übung stehen nur *present tense* und *past tense* zur Auswahl. Allerdings musst du dich auch zwischen *simple form* und *progressive form* entscheiden!

1. Where is Mr Speckler? – Behind the house. He (teach) the boys how to fly a kite.
2. While you (shop) this morning, someone (come) and (leave) this note.
3. In Arab countries women often (wear) veils and long dresses. (veil = Schleier)
4. When I (arrive) at the meeting, one of the guests (speak) and all the people (listen).
5. I (not go) out today because it (rain) and I (not have) an umbrella.
6. (you, love) Maggie? – No. I (like) her but I (not love) her.
7. After preparing lunch, mum (go) into the garden to see what everybody (do). Dad (plant) some flowers, James (mow) the lawn and "Tiger" (play) with his rubber ball.
8. Yesterday we (have) a family meeting, but I (not want) to meet my cousin Don. So I (leave) the room when he (arrive).
9. It (snow) this morning when I (look) out of the window.
10. We (get) to know many interesting people while we (travel) through India.

36 Jetzt kommt auch noch *present perfect* dazu. Also, du hast die Wahl: *present tense, past tense* oder *present perfect*?

1. When I (be) at school, we (read) a lot of books and stories by Jack London. I (enjoy) them very much, especially "Call of the Wild". (you, read) any of his books yet?
2. Yesterday, on the train to school, we suddenly (notice) that we (move) in the wrong direction.
3. Who (make) this terrible noise? – That's Mr Pitt. He (listen) to his radio, but he (not hear) well and so he (turn) the volume up all the way. (volume = Lautstärke)
4. How (you, usually, get) to school, Daniel? – Well, normally I (walk), but tomorrow dad (drive) me.
5. Here are your shoes, Margaret. I (just, clean) them. You always (put) them away without cleaning them!
6. Last Saturday Susanne (have) an accident. She (fall) and (hurt) her elbow while she (balance) on the garden wall.
7. Mr Peters (be) our bank manager. He (be) here for more than three years.
8. Look, Jack (wear) his new T-shirt. It's great, isn't it?
9. Uncle Max (wear) the same old hat for years. He (love) it, I guess.
10. At five o'clock this morning I (still, sleep). I usually (get) up at 6:30.

37 Vorsicht, Falle! *Present perfect* oder *past*? Denke daran: „Verbindung mit der Gegenwart" oder „abgeschlossen und vorbei". Bei einigen Sätzen musst du dich auch noch zwischen *since* und *for* entscheiden.

1. I (like) books and films since/for I was four years old.
2. When Maria (be) a little girl, she (love) playing with dolls.
3. Uncle Willie (live) in Australia since/for fifteen years. He (be) back only three times in all those years.
4. I (meet) Barbara when we (be) in school together. That (be) over ten years ago. This means I (know) her for a long time now, and after all these years we are still good friends.
5. What's your favourite subject? – Geography, I think. – Really? I (hate) geography since/for the first lesson.

6. What's the matter, Tina? What's worrying you? – Well, I (lose) my bus pass and now I can't go home. – When (you, find) out? – About ten minutes ago. I know I still (have) it when I (leave) school.
7. Hi, Mrs Baker. Can I speak with Sarah, please? – Hello, Chris. I'm sorry you can't; she (go) away on a short holiday for the next three days. She (leave) yesterday after work.
8. I (never, see) a more fascinating picture than "Mona Lisa" before. – Where (you, see) it? – In Paris, at the Louvre.

38

Jetzt kommen auch noch *past perfect* und die *future tenses* dazu. Du hast also die Qual der Wahl zwischen *present tense, past, present perfect, past perfect* und *future tenses*!

1. What (Harry, do) with a ladder? – He (climb) on the roof of the garden shed (= Gartenhütte).
2. Molly (try) on hats all morning. How boring!
3. We (do) twenty-five sentences in this lesson. That's enough!
4. We always (write) so much in our maths lesson.
5. Don't cry, Sally! We (ask) daddy for help and everything (be) alright again.
6. After Paul (call) his parents last night, he (go) to bed.
7. Sylvia and Jack (take) a long walk every evening. They usually (have) their dog with them.
8. Where's Helen? – Upstairs. I think she (bathe) the baby.
9. The Rothman family (live) in this beautiful old house since 1648.
10. It (begin) to rain while I (work) in the garden this morning.
11. We (wait) for you for hours. Thank heavens you're okay. Where (you, be) all the time?
12. Look! Somebody (leave) the front door open! – I'm sure that (be) grandpa. He always (forget) to shut the door.
13. The clouds are getting darker and darker. It (rain) soon. – Great! It (not rain) for three weeks now. Everybody (wait) for that rain!
14. What (you, eat)? Your lips are purple. – Really? Only some blueberries. Dad and I (pick) them ourselves. They are excellent. (you, want) to try some, too? – Yes, please. Blueberries (always, be) my favourites.

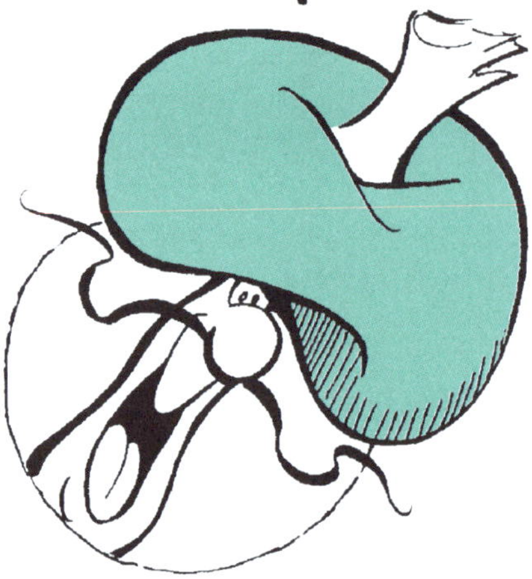

DENKMÜTZE

Hast du Schwierigkeiten, in der Schule gut hinzuhören und alles zu verstehen?

Die Denkmütze ist besonders vor Unterrichtsbeginn nützlich: Entfalte sanft deine Ohren. Beginne oben und massiere am Ohrrand entlang nach unten. Ziehe sanft an den Ohrläppchen. Wiederhole diese Bewegung von oben nach unten 10-mal. Wenn du gähnen musst, öffne dabei bitte den Mund so weit du kannst.

Wiederholung der Übung: 10-mal

Die *if*-Sätze (Bedingungssätze)

Die folgenden Formen sind dir bereits bekannt:

☆ der Fall der Wirklichkeit:

a If it rains the streets are wet

b *If it **rains,*** *the streets **will be** wet.*

↓ ↓

present tense *future (will + base form)*

☆ der Fall der Möglichkeit:

*If it **rained,*** *the streets **would be** wet.*

↓ ↓

past tense *conditional present (would + base form)*

Immer häufiger zu hören und zu lesen, aber von manchen Lehrern noch immer nicht gern gesehen:

*If it **would rain**, the streets **would be** wet.*

Vor blinder Nachahmung wird abgeraten! Erst mit dem Lehrer/der Lehrerin besprechen!!!

Und jetzt versuche dich zu erinnern! Denke scharf nach und überlege logisch:

- Welcher Satz ist der Hauptsatz?
- Welcher Satz ist der „if"-Satz?
- Welcher Satz ist die Bedingung? („wenn"-Satz)
- Welcher Satz ist die Folge? („dann"-Satz)

39

Daher am Anfang eine Übung zur Wiederholung! Bilde zuerst nur den Fall der Wirklichkeit (Sätze 1–6) und dann nur den Fall der Möglichkeit (Sätze 7–12).

example: Mary (get) ten pounds if she sells her old bike. →
Mary will get ten pounds if she sells her old bike.

If Sascha (go) home now, he would meet his brother. →
If Sascha went home now, he would meet his brother.

1. If it (be) too hot, we will stop and get a cool drink.
2. If you study hard in future, you (pass) your exam.
3. If you go on talking like that, we (throw) you out.
4. If you don't do as I tell you, you (be) sorry.
5. I'm sure Benny (come) if you wait a little longer.
6. You (not catch) the last train if you don't take a taxi now.
7. If it (rain) today, I would stay at home.
8. If I (see) Jane, I would tell her about your problem.
9. If you (find) a lot of money, would you keep it?
10. My father (not be) out of work if his firm made more money.
11. We would be very happy if our team (win) today.
12. If the Professor (speak) clearly, we would understand him better.

Wenn du alle Übungen richtig hast und dich wirklich sicher fühlst, dann kannst du weitermachen. Wenn nicht, dann arbeite die Übungen bitte noch einmal durch. („Wenn nicht, dann . . .!" ist übrigens ein sehr schöner Bedingungssatz!)

Der Fall der Unwirklichkeit oder Unmöglichkeit

Wir wollen natürlich nicht nur altbekannte Dinge wiederholen, sondern uns auch neuen Dingen zuwenden.

Lies dir das folgende Beispiel durch und du wirst verstehen, warum man die Bezeichnung „Unwirklichkeit" oder „Unmöglichkeit" gewählt hat:

If it ***had rained,***	*the streets* ***would have been*** *wet.*
↓	↓
past perfect tense	*conditional perfect (second conditional)* (*would have* + 3. Grundform)

Was wird hier beschrieben?
Wenn es geregnet **hätte, dann wären** die Straßen nass gewesen.
Es hat aber nicht geregnet, und die Straßen sind daher auch nicht nass. Das heißt, es ist unmöglich, dass die Straßen nass sind, denn es hat ja nicht geregnet. Die Situation ist unwirklich, weil die Bedingung nicht erfüllt wurde und die Folge somit nicht mehr eintreten kann.

Am Beispielsatz hast du gesehen, welche Zeiten und Formen du zur Bildung des Falls der Unmöglichkeit heranziehen musst:

R

[if] past perfect tense **+** ***conditional perfect (second conditional)***
(had + 3. Grundform) ***(would have + 3. Grundform)***

40 Diese Übung ist ein ganz einfacher Grammatikdrill. Er soll dir helfen, dich an die „neuen" Formen zu gewöhnen. Bilde mit den folgenden Personen und Verben jeweils *past perfect tense* und *conditional perfect*.

example: Peter (write) a letter. →
Peter had written a letter. (past perfect)
Peter would have written a letter. (conditional perfect)

1. we (run) faster
2. Andy (win) a prize
3. the children (be) late
4. you (not forget) your keys
5. I (think) about it
6. Dad (go) to bed earlier
7. the fire (break) out
8. we (not be) there in time

Die folgenden Beispiele helfen dir beim Erkennen der richtigen Zeit:

☆ *If Peter* ***(save)*** *all his money, he* ***would have bought*** *a new bike.* →

Der Hauptsatz mit *conditional perfect* ist vorgegeben; daher setzt du im „*if*"-Satz *past perfect* ein;

If Peter had saved *all his money, he* ***would have bought*** *a new bike.*

☆ *If Mary had done her work better, she (go) swimming on Sunday.* →

Der „*if*-"Satz mit ***past perfect*** ist vorgegeben; daher setzt du im Hauptsatz ***conditional perfect*** ein.

If Mary had done her work better, she would have gone *swimming on Sunday.*

Logo und klaro??? Dann geht's nach einer ans Üben!

41 Fall der Unmöglichkeit! Setze die richtigen Zeitstufen ein!

example: If Bob (take) his pills, he would have been well sooner. →
If Bob had taken his pills, he would have been well …

If Claire had met her dad, she (ask) him for money. →
If Claire had met her dad, she would have asked him …

1. If Susan (learn) the poem, she would have known the answer.
2. If I (not tell) Tim your address, he wouldn't have found you.
3. I would have found my keys if I (look) more carefully.
4. It would have been better if you (go) home earlier.
5. John (come) to your party if you had invited him.
6. I (not lose) my telescope if I had left it at home.
7. If I had known the boy's name, I (not tell) you.
8. We (catch) the train if we had left earlier.
9. I (win) the prize if I had worked harder.
10. She (hit) him if he had said a word.
11. The bird (die) if you had caught it.
12. Charlie (kiss) Susi if he had not been so shy. (shy = schüchtern)

42 Alles oder fast alles klar? Hoffentlich, denn jetzt wird die Sache etwas schwieriger! Beide Verben stehen in Klammer, und du musst entscheiden, wo *past perfect* und wo *conditional perfect* hingehören! Setze also in die richtige Zeitstufe im Fall der Unmöglichkeit.

example: If Sue (go) on holiday to Austria, she (learn) how to ski. →
If Sue had gone on …, she would have learned how …

1. I (pay) for the hamburgers if you (want) some.
2. My parents (say) no if they (know) that it was so dangerous.
3. If I (have) more money with me, I (buy) four computer games.
4. The water in the pool (freeze) if it (be) a little colder last night.
5. If dad (not forget) his wallet, he (buy) me a CD.
6. I (come) in time if my car (not break) down.
7. If you (not come) home now, we (call) the police.
8. If we (stay) longer in Portsmouth, we (visit) the Submarine Museum.
9. Mum (not be) so disappointed if we (not tell) her all those lies.
10. If you (wait) a little longer, you (see) the Queen!

43

Jetzt werden die „Fälle" gemischt! Alle drei stehen zur Auswahl: „Wirklichkeit", „Möglichkeit" und „Unmöglichkeit". Du musst aber kein Hellseher sein, um den richtigen Fall zu erkennen, denn:
Die gesuchte Zeitstufe ergibt sich immer zwingend aus der angegebenen!

1. If you ring the bell, somebody (answer) it.
2. If Bert (see) you, he would have talked to you.
3. You (find) your ticket if you had looked into your pockets.
4. You (fall) ill if you eat so much. (to fall ill = krank werden)
5. What (happen) if the door had not been opened?
6. If Chris asked you for a cigarette, (you, give) him one?
7. If you (buy) that big car, you would need a lot of money.
8. (you, change) the colour of your hair if I asked you to do so?
9. If you give me the letter, I (post) it for you.
10. (you, post) the letter if I had given it to you?

1

Es geht zunächst nur um den Fall der Unmöglichkeit (du weißt schon: *past perfect tense* + *conditional perfect*!). Du musst erkennen, wo welche Form passt! Pro richtiger Form gibt es einen Punkt „Belohnung"!

❍❍ 1. I (read) the letter if I (know) that it was from you.
❍❍ 2. If Tony (not help) me in the garden, I (not finish) my work in time.
❍❍ 3. If you (not tell) me about Maxwell's birthday, I (forget) it.
❍❍ 4. We (catch) the earlier train if Mary (found) her purse.
❍❍ 5. Dinner (be) fine if the meat (not be) cold.
❍❍ 6. If the weather (not change), we (reach) the top of the mountain.
❍❍ 7. If I (ask) you for help, (you, say) yes or no?
❍❍ 8. What (you, do) if you (win) in the lottery?

Du solltest auf alle Fälle mindestens 12 Punkte erreichen! Wenn's weniger sind, arbeite das Kapitel noch einmal durch, bevor du zur Abschlussübung weitergehst.

2

Und hier ist sie, die Abschlussprüfung; das große Finale mit allen drei „Fällen". Du musst erkennen, um welchen Fall es sich bei den einzelnen Beispielen handelt, und dann die passende Form des Verbs einsetzen. *Good luck!*

❍ 1. If Jenny (be) older she wouldn't have done such a silly thing.
❍ 2. I'm sure I (find) them if they had waited for me.
❍ 3. We would buy a bigger screen if it (not be) so expensive.
❍ 4. I (enjoy) the film much more if the music had not been so loud.
❍ 5. Our dog (run) away if she had not been tied to the dog-house. (to tie = anbinden)
❍ 6. If you don't put on your cap you (catch) cold.
❍ 7. The old woman would have been hit if the car (not stop) so quickly.
❍ 8. If you had a million dollars, what (you, do)?
❍ 9. They (not find) our house if we don't send them a plan.
❍ 10. If Tom is late again, (we, start) without him?
❍ 11. I (not wear) a coat if the sun was shining.
❍ 12. I'm sure we (visit) more sights if we had stayed in London longer.
❍ 13. If we (bring) something to eat, we would have had a picnic.
❍ 14. My friends would be very disappointed if they (lose) this match.
❍ 15. If you (go) to New York, you will meet lots of interesting people.

Das war's! Hast du alles richtig? ***Congratulations! You're the best!***

Die indirekte Rede

Billy says, "I want to go home."

Das ist **„direkte Rede"**. Mit ihr drückst du direkt und **ohne Veränderung** aus, was Billy gesagt hat.

Beachte, dass **im Englischen** – anders als im Deutschen – nach dem Zeitwort der Redeeinleitung (*. . . says . . .)* **ein Beistrich** (Komma) gesetzt wird. Weiter geht es in beiden Sprachen mit **Anführungszeichen**. Im Englischen werden alle Anführungszeichen **"oben"** gesetzt.

Wenn du jemand mitteilen möchtest, was jemand anderer sagt oder gesagt hat, verwendest du **„Indirekte Rede"**. Auf Englisch heißt sie ***"indirect speech"*** oder ***"reported speech"***. Wenn du eine Rede wiedergibst, verwendest du sie normalerweise, ohne nachzudenken.

Das ist nicht nur besserer Stil, sondern es kommt auch in der Alltagssprache viel häufiger vor:

*Billy **says** that he wants to go home.*
*Billy **said** that he wanted to go home.*

*Billy **asks** where he can put his shoes.*
*Billy **asked** where he could put his shoes.*

*Billy **tells** us to come to his place at four.*
*Billy **told** us to come to his place at four.*

Aussagen in „*indirect speech*"

Bei der Bildung der *indirect (reported) speech* im Englischen ist das **Zeitwort der Redeankündigung** *(verb of saying, reporting verb)* von allergrößter Bedeutung!

A

Wichtige Verben in diesem Zusammenhang sind:

remember (sich erinnern)
complain (sich beklagen)
report (berichten)
explain (erklären)
say
tell *(me, . . .)*
think
write
shout

reporting verb in present tense

Wenn das ***reporting verb in present tense*** steht, dann gibt es keinen Unterschied in den Zeitstufen zwischen der direkten und der indirekten Rede; **die Zeiten *(tenses)* verändern sich nicht.**

*Billy says, "I **want** to go home."* → *Billy says (that) he **wants** to go home.*

!

☆ Etwas anderes ändert sich allerdings schon: die Fürwörter *(personal and possessive pronouns).*

Billy sagt von sich: *"**I** want to go home."*

Wenn dieser Satz in die indirekte Rede gesetzt wird, dann spricht aber nicht mehr Billy selbst, sondern irgendjemand erzählt, was Billy gesagt hat.

Es heißt daher richtig: ***Billy** says (that) **he** wants to go home.*

Bei unserem Mustersatz steht das Wort *that* in Klammer: ***(that)***. Das hat einen einfachen Grund: Wenn du willst, kannst du es verwenden; es wird aber in der modernen Umgangssprache meist weggelassen.

Die Veränderungen von *personal and possessive pronoun* ergeben sich daraus, **wer mit wem über wen spricht**. Am einfachsten kommst du dahinter, wenn du dir vorstellst, jemand spricht mit dir, und du erzählst dann weiter, was dieser „jemand" zu dir gesagt hat!

44 Diese Veränderung der *pronouns* kannst du jetzt gleich üben! Verwandle also die folgenden Sätze in die indirekte Rede.

example: Pat says, "I want to have a new bike." →
Pat says (that) he wants to have a new bike.

1. Susi says, "I want to have the new CD for my birthday."
2. Freddy says to his teacher, "I have not done my homework, sir."
3. Anne tells her mother, "Carl wants to visit me today."
4. Mum calls to her son Teddy, "You must be home at six o'clock."
5. Mr Daniels writes to his sister, "I will go on holiday in August."
6. Lucas says, "I spent my Easter holidays in London."

45 Bei dieser Übung musst du die Pronomen sinngemäß verändern! Bilde wieder die indirekte Rede und achte dabei besonders auf die Personen! Vergiss nicht: Die Zeitstufen ändern sich nicht.

example: Susi tells me, "I saw you yesterday." →
Susi tells me (that) she saw me yesterday.

1. Fred says, "I have to talk to you."
2. Father says, "I have finished my work in the garden."
3. My sister says, "Mary wants to see you, mum."
4. Carla tells me, "My father does not know you."
5. Ms Jansen, our maths teacher, says to us, "I am proud of you, girls."
6. Granny says, "I have been thinking of you all morning."

Was für *personal pronouns* gilt, **gilt** – wie gesagt – **auch für *possessive pronouns*** (besitzanzeigende Fürwörter oder Possessivpronomen). Das heißt, auch *my, your, his, . . .* ändern sich sinngemäß.
Es kommt wieder darauf an, wer mit wem über wen spricht.

46

Verwandle in die indirekte Rede und achte dieses Mal besonders auf die *possessive pronouns.*

example: Father says, "I haven't read my newspaper today." →
Father says (that) he hasn't read his newspaper today.

1. Marcello says, "I would like to see your Star Wars models."
2. Mr and Mrs Cooper tell us, "We enjoyed our holiday very much."
3. Colin says, "Yesterday I saw Betty with her new bike."
4. Doris complains (= klagt), "I can't find my new pen."
5. Uncle Edward thinks, "Someone has been in my garden."
6. Charlie tells Mac, "You can have my umbrella as long as it's raining."
7. The Johnsons write, "We met your uncle on our tour through France."
8. Grandfather remembers, "I got my first bicycle when I was seventeen."

Wenn man einen Satz von der direkten Rede in die indirekte Rede bringt und das Zeitwort der Redeankündigung *(verb of saying, reporting verb)* dabei in *present tense* steht,

- ☆ **ändern sich** die ***personal und possessive pronouns*** je nach dem Sinn des Satzes;
- ☆ **bleiben** die **Zeitstufen** der direkten Rede **unverändert**.

reporting verb in past tense

*Billy **said**, "I **want** to go home." → Billy **said** he **wanted** to go home.*
Was ist passiert?
Wenn das ***verb of saying*** in ***past tense*** steht, dann ändern sich neben den bekannten Dingen auch und vor allem **die Zeitstufen**.

Warum sich die Zeitstufen ändern, ist eigentlich leicht zu verstehen:

☆ In der direkten Rede sagt „Mister X" etwas zu „Mister Y".
In der indirekten Rede teilt „Mr Y" das, was „Mr X" gesagt hat, dem „Mister Z" mit.

☆ Mr Y sagt: *Mr X **tells** me (that) he wants to see me soon.*
Wenn also das *reporting verb* in *present tense* steht (. . . **tells** . . .), dann heißt das:

- Mr X spricht jetzt und hier;
- Mr Y hört dies jetzt und hier;
- und er erzählt es Mr Z jetzt und hier weiter.

☆ Steht das ***reporting verb*** in ***past tense,*** so heißt das:

- Unser Mr X hat irgendwann und irgendwo etwas gesagt;
- Mr Y hat dies irgendwann und irgendwo gehört oder erfahren;
- und hat es Mr Z irgendwann und irgendwo weitergesagt.

! ☆ Daraus folgt: **Die Zeitstufen, aber auch die Orts- und Zeitangaben müssen sich ändern,** denn sonst wird der Inhalt der direkten Rede nicht so wiedergegeben, wie er gemeint war.

R

Was verändert sich nun alles bei ***reporting verb in past tense***?

1. ***personal and possessive pronouns:*** das persönliche Fürwort und das besitzanzeigende Fürwort (wie bereits geübt)
2. ***tense:*** die Zeitstufe
3. ***place:*** die Ortsangabe
4. ***time:*** die Zeitangabe

Die Änderung der Zeitstufen *(change of tenses)*

present tense → past tense

*Martin said, "I **like** your baseball cap." →*
*Martin said (that) he **liked** my baseball cap.*

47

Versuche es gleich einmal selbst! Bei den ersten Sätzen geht es nur um den Wechsel von *present tense* zu *past tense*.

1. Mrs Miller said, "You live in a very fine house."
2. The stranger said, "I don't know where to find a doctor."
3. Charlie shouted, "Maxwell and Susi are in the swimming pool!"
4. The driver explained, "St. Paul's is the biggest church in England." (to explain = erklären)

present perfect → past perfect

Mother said, "We ***have got*** *a letter from grandmother." →*
Mother said (that) we **had got** *a letter from grandmother.*

48 Du bist wieder an der Reihe! Achte diesmal auf den Wechsel von *present perfect tense* zu *past perfect tense*.

1. The Johnsons reported, "We haven't been lucky with the weather."
2. Mike told me, "I have seen this show before."
3. Isabel said, "I have fallen in love with the nicest boy in town."
4. Dad shouted, "You've brought the wrong key."

past → past perfect

Tim told us, "We ***did not find*** *the station." →*
Tim told us (that) they **had not found** *the station.*

49 Jetzt musst du nur auf den Wechsel von *past tense* zu *past perfect tense* achten. (Du erinnerst dich: *had + past participle*.)

1. Carl told me, "I met Julia in kindergarten."
2. Martina remembered, "As a child I played Monopoly a lot."
3. Theo and Claudia reported, "We saw an accident on our way home from school."
4. The driver said to the policeman, "I did not notice the red light." (to notice = bemerken)

future tense → conditional present (first conditional)

The tourist guide said, "Your tour ***will start*** *in five minutes".*
The tourist guide said (that) our tour **would start** *in five minutes.*

50 Einmal geht's noch! *Future tense (will)* wird zu *conditional present (first conditional; would).*

1. Dad said, "We'll go to Spain again in summer."
2. Samantha told me, "My parents will call your parents on Saturday."
3. Tina said, "I'll have a big party at my place in a few weeks."
4. Maggie promised, "I won't tell my mother about you!"
   (to promise = versprechen)

A

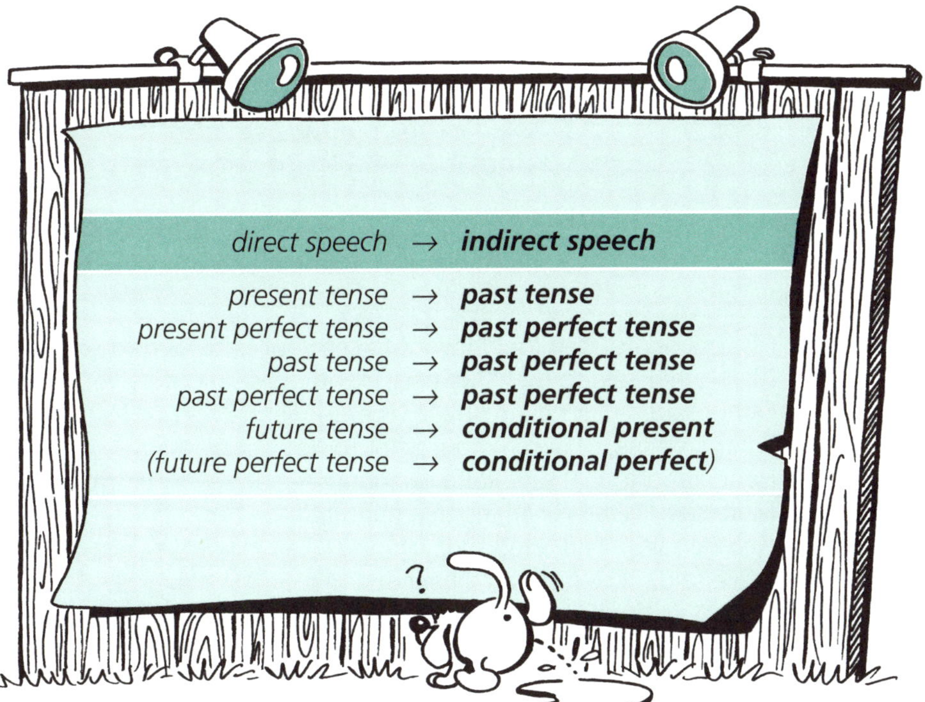

direct speech	→	***indirect speech***
present tense	→	***past tense***
present perfect tense	→	***past perfect tense***
past tense	→	***past perfect tense***
past perfect tense	→	***past perfect tense***
future tense	→	***conditional present***
(future perfect tense	→	***conditional perfect)***

Die Änderung der Orts- und Zeitangaben *(change of place and time)*

A

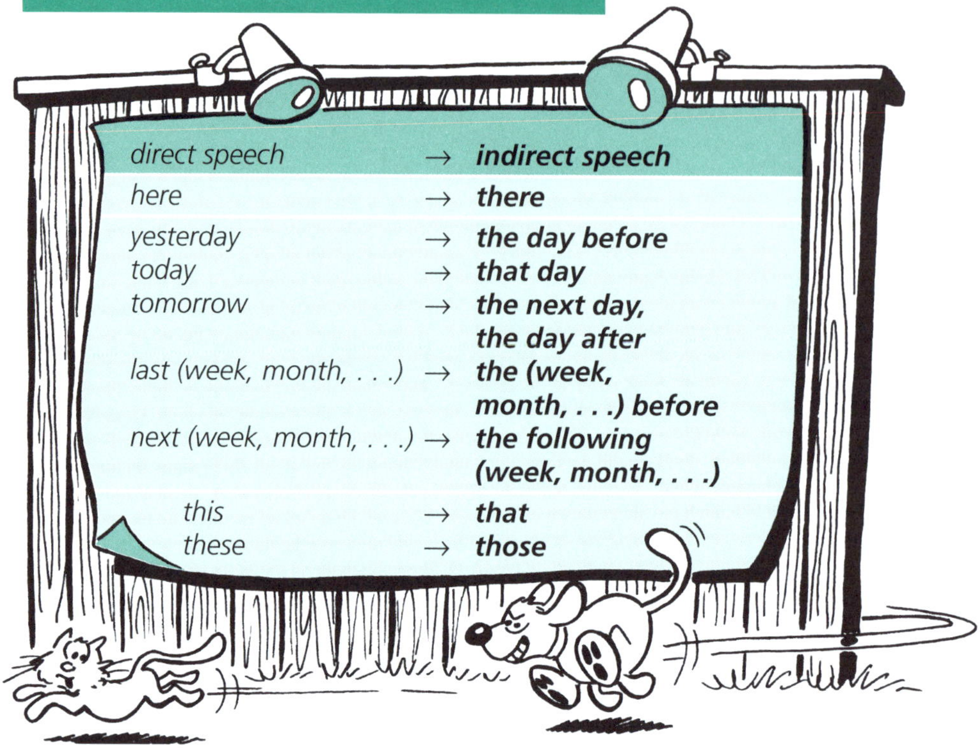

direct speech	→	***indirect speech***
here	→	***there***
yesterday	→	***the day before***
today	→	***that day***
tomorrow	→	***the next day, the day after***
last (week, month, . . .)	→	***the (week, month, . . .) before***
next (week, month, . . .)	→	***the following (week, month, . . .)***
this	→	***that***
these	→	***those***

Wenn du in der direkten Rede die Zeitangabe ***now*** vorfindest, so kannst du sie in der indirekten Rede ruhig weglassen!

Ein Beispiel: *Dad said, "We have to go **now**!"* →
Dad said (that) we had to go.

51 Die folgenden Übungen enthalten alles bisher Besprochene. Sie führen dich vom Einfachen zum Schwierigen. Wandle also wieder in die indirekte Rede um:

1. Mr Green informed me, "I want to see your parents next week."
2. My brother said to me, "My new friend does not know you."
3. Father said, "Our new manager lives in Vienna."
4. Frank told me, "I don't know what to do."
5. Henry reported, "I saw Petra yesterday."
6. Mum said, "Fred is coming in a minute."
7. George said, "I am tired today."
8. Willie said, "I've just had a haircut."

Gehe erst zur nächsten Übung, wenn du alle Sätze korrekt gemacht und auch verstanden hast. Diese Selbstkontrolle ist sehr wichtig!

52

Weiter geht's wie bisher!

1. Aunt Pauline wrote us, "I'll arrive next week."
2. Paul said, "I don't know what my brother is going to play on the piano."
3. Grandpa said, "I think I'm ill."
4. Cissy told me, "I fell down the stairs."
5. Dad said, "I must call my boss as soon as I can."
6. Harry said to George, "This car belongs to me."
7. Mum said, "I'll come when I have done the washing up."
8. I said, "I have never done this before."

PAUSE

1

Achtung! Der erste Punktebewerb! Verwandle die folgenden Sätze in die indirekte Rede. Beachte alle bereits gelernten und geübten Feinheiten, und es kann nichts schief gehen!

❍ 1. Mr Hammond said, "Sheila is a nice girl, but she wears strange clothes."
❍ 2. I told them, "I am very late today."
❍ 3. Mum said, "I'll leave the shopping bags in my car."
❍ 4. My teacher said, "Mary, you haven't done your homework for today."
❍ 5. The doctor said, "You must stay in bed for a couple of days."
❍ 6. Peter said on the phone, "I will be at home in two hours if the train isn't late again."
❍ 7. Donna said, "Yesterday was the last time I saw Peter."
❍ 8. I promised my parents, "I won't do it again."
❍ 9. Susan said, "I went to London by train last week."
❍ 10. Uncle Pierre said, "I am leaving Paris tomorrow."
❍ 11. My friends said, "We had to go home at five o'clock."
❍ 12. Judy said, "I'll call you back in a minute."
❍ 13. Mum said, "Sally will come home as soon as it gets dark."
❍ 14. Sandy said, "I haven't got the time to answer your letters."
❍ 15. Sam said, "I'm sorry I didn't come last week, but I will come tomorrow."
❍ 16. Our teacher said, "We are having a holiday tomorrow."

16 oder 15 Punkte: **Hervorragend!**
14 oder 13 richtige Antworten: **Gute Arbeit!**
Bei 12 oder weniger Punkten solltest du noch **weiterüben**.
Bei weniger als 10 Punkten heißt es: **Zurück an den Start** und das Kapitel „Indirekte Rede" nochmals durcharbeiten!

Fragen in der indirekten Rede

Du musst grundsätzlich zwischen diesen beiden Arten von Fragen unterscheiden.

Entscheidungsfragen

Das sind Fragen, die bei der **Antwort eine Entscheidung** verlangen. Man muss also zwischen **ja oder nein** wählen:

> *"Do you want to go to the cinema with me?"* →
> *"**Yes,** I do!"* oder *"**No,** I don't!"*

Die **indirekte Frage** sieht dann so aus:

> *Tony asked me, "**Do you want to go** to the cinema with me?"* →
> *Tony asked me **if I wanted to go** to the cinema with him.*

Die Entscheidungsfrage besitzt in der direkten Rede kein Fragewort. Sie muss also in der indirekten Rede so etwas Ähnliches wie ein **Fragewort** bekommen. In unserer Sprache wäre das **„ob"**:

Tony fragte mich, **ob** ich mit ihm ins Kino gehen will (wolle).

TiPP Im Englischen heißt „ob" entweder ***if*** oder ***whether.*** Beide Wörter bedeuten dasselbe; du kannst entscheiden, welches der beiden du verwendest. (Wir verwenden in der Folge meistens das kürzere *if.*)

Was hat sich bei der Umwandlung der direkten Frage in die indirekte Frage geändert?

1. Die Zeitstufen, die Pronomen (Fürwörter) und die Orts- und Zeitangaben (aber das weißt du ja schon).
2. Zwischen die Redeankündigung und die indirekte Rede schiebt sich das Fragewort ***if*** oder ***whether.***
3. Aus dem Fragesatz *"Do you want to go to the cinema with me?"* wird der Aussagesatz *"Tony asked me if I wanted to go . . ."*

Besonders wichtig ist dabei Punkt 3. Er sagt, dass alles, was durch die Frage in den Satz kam, wieder wegfällt. Daher fehlen in der indirekten Frage auch das Stützwort *do* und das Fragezeichen!

Die indirekte Frage ist kein Fragesatz, sondern ein Aussagesatz!

Das sind die wichtigsten ***reporting verbs*** der indirekten Frage.

Bilde die indirekte Frage und beachte dabei die oben genannten drei Punkte!

example: John asked his dad, "Do you know Mary's address?" →
John asked his dad if he knew Mary's address.

1. Herbert asked me, "Do you know her name?"
2. Uncle Jim asked father, "Did you see the fight yesterday?"
3. My friend wanted to know, "Does Sally play tennis?"
4. Our neighbours asked us, "Do you want to use our telephone?"
5. Mum asked, "Did you lay the table, Jenny?"
6. Mac asked Charlie, "Do you like Susi?"
7. Mary wanted to know, "Did Bill call yesterday?"
8. Mum asked grandpa, "Does your coat keep you warm?"

Erst weitermachen, wenn du (fast) alle richtig hast! Vergleiche mit dem Lösungsheft!

Der <u>Fragesatz</u> ***"Are you afraid of dogs?"*** wird durch die Rückführung der Wortstellung zu ***"She was afraid of dogs."*** wieder zu einem <u>Aussagesatz</u>.

54

Das kannst du gleich selbst üben. Wandle die folgenden Sätze in indirekte Fragen um. Achte diesmal besonders auf die Rückführung der Wortstellung (Subjekt – Prädikat)!

example: Mum asked us, "<u>Has Ted</u> made his bed?" →
Mum asked us if Ted had made his bed.

1. My sister asked me, "Are you doing your homework?"
2. Mr Featherstonehaugh asked me, "Have you seen my new car?"
3. Mum wanted to know, "Is the milk cold enough?"
4. My friend wanted to know, "Will you come at nine?"
5. Our teacher asked Fred, "Can you jump higher than Brian?"
6. Jack asked Jill, "Will you marry me in September?"
7. The policeman wanted to know, "Have you seen this man before?"
8. I asked my neighbour, "Will you keep my key until tomorrow?"

55

Weiter geht es mit „gemischter Kost"!

1. Monica asked me, "Will you show me your presents tomorrow?"
2. I asked Marcus, "Did you finish your model plan yesterday?"
3. My friend asked me, "Has your dad given up smoking?"
4. My teacher asked us, "Did you write all the answers?"
5. The doctor asked me, "Do you sleep well at night?"
6. I asked the tourist, "Do you understand me?"
7. Grandma asked me, "Was the bus full?"
8. Mum asked dad, "Have you finished cooking?"

Ergänzungsfragen

Das sind Fragen, die man nicht einfach mit „Ja" oder „Nein" beantworten kann. Hier dient die **Antwort** in irgendeiner Form **als Ergänzung**.

*Betty asked Patricia, "**Where** are you going?"*
*Patricia answered, **"To the cinema."*** (→ Ortsergänzung)

Ergänzungsfragen werden durch ein Fragewort eingeleitet.
Das **Fragewort wird** in der indirekten Rede **beibehalten**!

*Betty asked Patricia, "**Where** are you going?"*
*Betty asked Patricia **where** she was going.*

Was hat sich bei der Umwandlung der direkten Frage in die indirekte Frage geändert?

1. die Zeitstufen;
2. die Orts- und Zeitangaben;
3. die Wortstellung (wie schon bei der Ergänzungsfrage).

Was ändert sich nicht?

! **4.** Das Fragewort der direkten Rede bleibt erhalten.

56

Bilde die indirekten Fragen. Verwende das Fragewort der direkten Frage weiter.

example: Henry asked me, "How did you meet Mr Carter?" →
Henry asked me how I had met Mr Carter.

1. I asked Jane, "When did Gerry leave?"
2. Willie asked me, "Where will you be tomorrow?"
3. Mum asked us, "Where are you going?"
4. Dad wanted to know, "Where did I put my records?"
5. The detective asked me, "What do you know about it?"
6. I asked the girl, "How old are you?"
7. Mrs Shepherd asked me, "What did you want to say?"
8. Mum asked my brother, "When do you want to get up tomorrow?"

57

Nimm dir diese Übung erst vor, wenn du *exercise* 56 ohne Fehler gemacht hast. Es geht um die gleiche Sache wie vorhin!

1. Peter asked his dad, "What are we going to do in the zoo today?"
2. I asked the boys, "Why didn't you tell me about your problem?"
3. Mum asked Tony, "What have you learned in school today?"
4. The Jeffersons asked us, "When will you come again?"
5. I asked the assistant, "How much are the tin soldiers?"
6. I asked Maria, "Where can we meet tomorrow?"
7. The lady asked us, "Where are you from?"
8. The policeman wanted to know, "Whose car is this?"

2

Zeige, was du kannst – es geht um Punkte! Es zählen wieder nur vollkommen richtige Antworten. Du findest hier Ergänzungsfragen und Entscheidungsfragen gemischt vor. Bilde indirekte Fragen daraus!

❍ 1. I asked Mandy, "Have you been to the hairdresser's today?"
❍ 2. Sam asked me, "Which colour do you like best?"
❍ 3. Harry asked Frieda, "What did Mrs Wilson tell you about me?"
❍ 4. Susi asked Charlie, "Do you love me?"
❍ 5. Sandra wanted to know, "Did Thomas say anything?"
❍ 6. I asked Tony, "Has Sally come home yet?"
❍ 7. Miss Anderson asked us, "Why are you asking me silly questions?"
❍ 8. I wanted to know, "What is so interesting about the book?"
❍ 9. Mum asked us, "Why don't you try harder?"
❍ 10. The police asked me, "When did you meet Miss Brown?"
❍ 11. Mum's boss wanted to know, "Where did you learn English?"
❍ 12. Albert asked Judith, "Can you call me tomorrow morning?"

11 oder 12 Punkte: ***Splendid!!!***
9 oder 10 Punkte: ***Good!***
7 oder 8: ***Okay.***

Befehle, Bitten und Verbote

Der direkte Befehl (Bitte, Verbot) ist eine recht einfache Sache. Das hat drei Gründe:

- ☆ Ein Befehl lässt sich nur in *present tense* aussprechen.
- ☆ Ein Befehl richtet sich immer an die 2. Person *(you)*.
- ☆ Der indirekte Befehl wird einfach mit der **Nennform *(base form, infinitive)*** gebildet.

Dazu das gewohnte Beispiel:

My father said to me, "Come home at once!"
My father told me ***to come*** *home at once.*
(oder: *My father said* ***that I should*** *come home.* → eine Aussage)

Die **Bitte** unterscheidet sich vom Befehl nur im Ton, und den erkennt man an der Einleitung ***(reporting verb)***.

Father ***asked*** *me to come home at once.* = Er bat mich darum.
Father ***told*** *me to come at once.* = Er sagte, ich solle . . .

Ein **Verbot** bedeutet, dass man etwas **nicht tun** darf! In der indirekten Rede wird das Verbot mit der verneinten Nennform ***(negative infinitive)*** gebildet:

Mum said, "Don't play your music so loud!"
Mum told us ***not to play*** *our music so loud.*
(Mum said that we should not play our music so loud.)

Die wichtigsten ***reporting verbs*** sind ***tell*** und ***ask.***

58

Befehle, Bitten, Verbote – alles findest du hier! Bilde die indirekte Rede mit den angegebenen Sätzen. Wenn du bei einem Satz Smiley ☺ siehst, solltest du auch einen indirekten Aussagesatz bilden.

example: The coach said, "Do fifty push-ups and fifty sit-ups." ☺ →
The coach told us to do fifty push-ups and fifty sit-ups.
(The coach said we should do fifty push-ups and . . .)

1. The old man told us, "Go away!" ☺
2. Mr Mason said to us, "Copy the exercise into your books!"
3. Mum said to me, "Wash your hands, please!" (eine Bitte!)
4. I told my friends, "Run faster!" ☺
5. The teacher said to the class, "Sit down!"
6. Grandma said, "Don't climb on this tree!" ☺
7. Susi said to Charlie, "Don't go home now!"
8. Mr Smith said, "Please come in and sit down!"

59

Es geht fast genauso weiter, nur dieses Mal entscheidest du selbst, wer was zu wem sagt.

1. "Put out your cigar, please!"
2. "Shut up!"
3. "Brush your teeth!"
4. "Wait for me, please!"
5. "Eat it up!"
6. "Don't ask me what I don't know!"
7. "Sing with us, please!"
8. "Don't wait for me!"

60 Letzte Übungschance vor den Punktebewerben! Jetzt wird alles gemischt; Aussagen, Fragen (Entscheidungsfragen und Ergänzungsfragen), Befehle, Bitten und Verbote. Vergiss nicht, dass du einen Aussagesatz anders einleiten musst als einen Fragesatz oder einen Befehl!

example: "Do you have any questions? Ask me whatever you want!" → Martha asked me if I had any questions and told me to ask her whatever I wanted.

1. "Take it away! I don't like it."
2. "Why are you waiting? Henry has already gone home."
3. "Did Jack tell you about the film? Go and ask him about it!"
4. "Where did you spend your holiday? Tell me about it, please!"
5. "How do you like my new shoes? I bought them in Carnaby Street."
6. "Do you want another apple? They are so sweet."
7. "Where does Jenny live? I want to visit her next week."
8. "Will you ask Peter? Don't be so shy!"
9. "Vienna is wonderful. Have you been there?"
10. "Don't wait for us. We're going to be late."

61 Allerletzte Übung, bevor es Punkte gibt! Nütze deine Chance!

1. "When did you paint this picture? It is wonderful."
2. "Why don't you play with me? Do you think I'm too young?"
3. "Where did dad put the shopping list? Go and get it, please!"
4. "Take your feet off the table! Where do you think you are?"
5. "Where were you waiting for me? I was at the bus-stop."
6. "How do you feel? I'm alright."
7. "Tell Pamela to go home now. Her mum is already waiting."
8. "Wait for me, please. I can't run so fast."
9. "Play it again, Sam! I like this song so very much."
10. "Stop now! It's enough."

3

Jetzt geht's los! Du solltest die indirekte Rede schon gut beherrschen nach den vielen Übungen! Denke daran: Für die Punktebewertung zählen gnadenlos nur vollkommen richtige Sätze, also mit richtigem Zeitenwechsel, richtigen Pronomen, richtigen Orts- und Zeitangaben, usw., usw.

❍ 1. "What are you doing here? It's too late."
❍ 2. "Bring the book back! I am waiting for it."
❍ 3. "Don't jump from here, please! It's too dangerous."
❍ 4. "How did Anne sing? I told you she is wonderful."
❍ 5. "Come in, please! There is tea and cake for all of you."
❍ 6. "Don't play with the dog. She is ill."
❍ 7. "How much is it? I'll buy it."
❍ 8. "Go home now! It's late and your parents are waiting."
❍ 9. "Didn't I tell you not to come? I don't need you here."
❍ 10. "Mary wants to help you. Go and tell her you are ready!"
❍ 11. "Go to bed now, my dear. I'm coming soon."
❍ 12. "Stop that noise! The baby wants to sleep."

11 oder 12 Punkte: ***Splendid!!!***
9 oder 10 Punkte: ***Good!***
7 oder 8: ***Okay.***

4

Und jetzt ist unwiderruflich Schluss! Du hast das letzte Hindernis vor dir. Alles Gute! Du schaffst es sicher!

❍ 1. "Why did she leave you? You looked happy together."
❍ 2. "Where were you? I was waiting for you."
❍ 3. "Did you know that Charlie is getting married? I wasn't sure."
❍ 4. "Have you been waiting long? My car didn't start."
❍ 5. "They didn't throw him out. He left by himself."
❍ 6. "What do you think? Was I right?"
❍ 7. "Don't leave the house now. It is raining heavily."
❍ 8. "Do you think this is enough now? I do."
❍ 9. "You must not touch the controls. Do you understand?"
❍ 10. "Please sing for us, Jenny. You've got such a lovely voice."
❍ 11. "Mrs Thompson hasn't left her house in three days. Don't you think that's strange?"
❍ 12. "Put the bags on the floor, please. We'll put them away tomorrow."

11 oder 12 Punkte: ***Splendid!!!***
9 oder 10 Punkte: ***Good!***
7 oder 8: ***Okay.***

ZAUBERPUNKT

Du fühlst dich nicht wohl?
Es stresst dich, lernen zu müssen?
Du hast Heißhunger auf Süßes?

Die Energie deines Körpers ist zu niedrig. Da hilft dir der Zauberpunkt:
Du legst zwei Finger der linken Hand auf die Innenseite des rechten Handgelenks. Diesen Punkt massierst du 2-mal täglich 4 bis 12 Minuten und immer dann, wenn es dir nicht gut geht. Du wirst merken, wie das funktioniert. Wenn du an dieser Stelle die Energie aktivierst, verzichtet dein Körper auch freiwillig auf Süßigkeiten. Süßigkeiten sind Energiefresser!

Dauer der Übung: 4 bis 12 Minuten

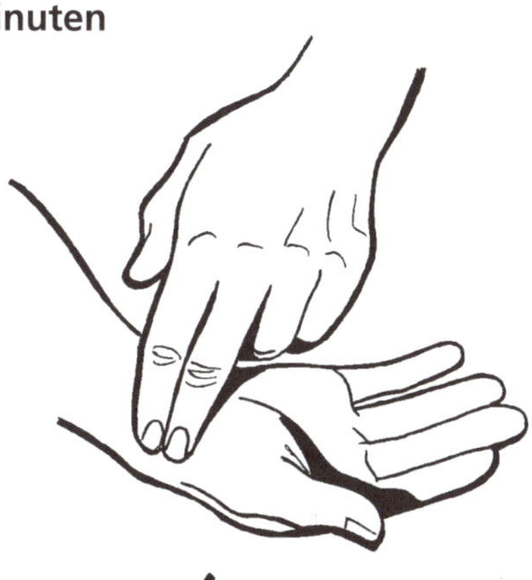

DAS EIGENSCHAFTSWORT

Im vorigen Schuljahr – und natürlich auch im Band „Durchstarten in Englisch für die 6. Schulstufe" – hast du die Grundlagen der Steigerung gelernt. Heuer kommen noch ein paar „Feinheiten" dazu, und selbstverständlich wird auch wiederholt!

Steigerung und Vergleich *(comparison)*

Wir kennen . . .

long	*long**er***	*long**est***
easy	*easi**er***	*easi**est***

expensive	***more** expensive*	***most** expensive*
boring	***more** boring*	***most** boring*

good	***better***	***best***
bad	***worse***	***worst***

Man sagt: „Wer rastet, der rostet." Damit dir das nicht auch passiert, wollen wir gleich mit einer leichten Wiederholungsübung beginnen.

62

Setze die angegebenen Eigenschaftswörter *(adjectives)* in die jeweils richtige Form.

example: Do you know the name of the (long) river in the world? →
Do you know the name of the **longest** river in the world?

This is the (interesting) book I have ever read. →
This is the **most interesting** book I have ever read.

1. A little spider is sometimes (frightening) than a big dog.
2. Mr F. is the (boring) teacher in the whole school.
3. I think Sabine is the (pretty) girl in our class.
4. A bikepath is usually (narrow) than a road. (bikepath = Radweg)
5. My English teacher thinks English is the (easy) thing on earth.
6. Most girls are (polite) than boys.
7. A computer is (expensive) than a pocket calculator (= Taschenrechner).
8. July and August are usually the (hot) months of the year.
9. Children usually have (little) money but (much) time than grown-ups. (grown-ups = Erwachsene)
10. Snowboarding is (expensive) than skiing.

Und nun zu den „neuen" Dingen der 7. Schulstufe:

- ☆ mehr über die unregelmäßige Steigerung
- ☆ die „zunehmende" Steigerung
- ☆ der Vergleich mit „je – desto"
- ☆ eine Warnung vor *adjectives,* die ähnlich aussehen, aber verschiedene Bedeutungen haben
- ☆ weitere Vergleiche

DIE UNREGELMÄSSIGE STEIGERUNG

Einige **unregelmäßige Adjektive** sind dir schon bekannt. Dieses Jahr wollen wir uns die Sache etwas näher ansehen.

Hier eine etwas genauere Liste mit wichtigen unregelmäßigen Adjektiven. Versuche dir einmal wirklich klar zu machen, was diese Wörter bedeuten, auch auf Deutsch, und wodurch sich ihre Bedeutung unterscheidet!

A

positive	***comparative***	***superlative***	**deutsche Bedeutung**
old	*older* *elder*	*oldest* *eldest*	alt (normale Bedeutung) älter, . . . (nur bei Familien-mitgliedern)
good *bad* *evil [i:vl]*	*better* *worse* *worse*	*best* *worst* *worst*	gut schlecht, böse böse, bösartig
well *ill*	*better* *worse*	*best* *worst*	gesund krank
many *much* *little*	*more* *more* *less*	*most* *most* *least [li:st]*	viele (mit Mehrzahl) viel (mit Einzahl) wenig (mit Einzahl)
little	*smaller*	*smallest*	klein
late	*later* *(the) latter*	*latest* *last*	spät letzterer – (der) letzte
near *far*	*nearer* *farther* *further*	*nearest* *next* *farthest* *(furthest)*	nahe, nächst(gelegen) (der) nächste in der Reihe weit (entfernt) weitere (z. B. Fragen, . . .)

Einige Beispiele zum Überlegen:

☆ *Bill and Tony are my friends. The* ***latter*** *is also my neighbour.*

Bill und Tony sind meine Freunde. **Letzterer** ist auch mein Nachbar. (Damit ist Tony gemeint, der „zuletzt Genannte", eben „letzterer".)

☆ *I have no* ***further*** *questions.*

Ich habe keine **weiteren** Fragen mehr.
(Das heißt, ich habe nicht vor, noch irgendwelche Fragen zu stellen; das war meine letzte Frage. Das hat natürlich mit Entfernung überhaupt nichts zu tun!)

63

Setze die richtigen unregelmäßigen Steigerungsformen ein. Schau ruhig in der Tabelle nach! Gut geschaut (aber nicht zum Nachbarn!) ist halb gewonnen!

example: Carina is my (old) sister. She is three years (old) than I. →
Carina is my elder sister. She is three years older than I.

1. Martin was not well yesterday, but he told me he was getting (good).
2. I know very little about South America, but my younger brother knows even (little) than I. (even = sogar)
3. The snow spread to the (far) end of our garden.
(to spread = sich ausbreiten)
4. We are waiting for (far) news from Uncle Harry.
5. Is everybody hungry? Let's go to "Antonio's Pizzeria"! – No, let's go to McDonald's! It's (near) than "Antonio's".
6. I fell ill last week, but instead of getting (good) I got (bad).
(to fall ill = krank werden; instead of = anstatt)

7. My new friend lives (far) away than I thought.
8. I was the (late) to finish the race because I was too slow.
9. As I get (old), I have (much) money but (little) time.
10. In most fairy tales the rich people are (evil) than the poor.
11. Charlie is the (little) boy in his class.
12. Which films do you like (good), horror films or adventure films? – I like (late) best.

1

Du solltest jetzt bereit sein für die erste Punkteübung. Sie enthält „Altbekanntes" und „Neues". Setze also die passenden Formen ein.

example: I like (cheap) clothes, because I feel (comfortable) in them. →
I like cheaper clothes, because I feel more comfortable in them.

❍❍ 1. The (near) shop was closed, so we went to the (near) one.
❍ 2. It's (nice) to play with friends than to work in the garden.
❍ 3. I had (little) money with me than I thought.
❍❍❍ 4. That was the (difficult) homework we ever had. I hope the (near) one will be (easy).
❍ 5. Henry finished (late) in the 100-meter sprint. I came in first.
❍ 6. We need (far) information before we can say yes or no.
❍ 7. "Who is (near)?" the dentist asked.
❍❍ 8. Sometimes reading a book is (interesting) than watching TV and sometimes it's (boring).
❍ 9. Which is (near), Berlin or Amsterdam?
❍ 10. This has been the (happy) day of my life.

Ab 12 richtigen Antworten: ***Most excellent!*** Weniger als 7: ***The least!***

☆ *Charlie says to Susi, "You are getting **prettier and prettier**."* – „Du wirst immer hübscher."

☆ *Father grew **more and more impatient**.*
Vater wurde immer ungeduldiger.

Im Englischen wird diese **Zunahme durch Wiederholung** ausgedrückt.
(Im Deutschen verwenden wir dafür das Wort **„immer"** mit dem Komparativ, das ist die erste Steigerungsstufe!)

64 Bilde die zunehmende Steigerung mit den folgenden Beispielen.

example: The team worked (hard) and won the championship. →
The team worked harder and harder and won . . .

The police was (interested) in the robbery. →
The police was more and more interested in the robbery.

1. The children sang (loud).
2. The class became (quiet).
3. The film got (horrifying).
4. Tony's face grew (long).
5. The little boy ran (far) into the wood.
6. With the help of "Durchstarten" Fred got (good) at English.
7. The money in my piggy-bank became (much).
8. The little pig grew (fat).

2 Bilde die zunehmende Steigerung! Du wirst sehen, mit der Zeit wird alles *easier and easier*!

❍ 1. With the years Caroline became (attractive).
❍ 2. Since last year petrol has got (expensive).
❍ 3. The wind was getting (cold) so that we went inside.
❍❍ 4. We drove (fast), so the city came (near).
❍ 5. Your questions are getting (intelligent) every minute!
❍ 6. There are (few) fish in the sea.
❍ 7. My headache is getting (bad).
❍❍ 8. I've (little) time for my hobbies but (much) work to do for school.
❍ 9. You're getting (old) but you're not getting cleverer.
❍ 10. Riding a bike in the city has become (dangerous).

Na, wie sieht's aus? Bei 8 bis 9 richtigen Antworten: ***You're okay!*** Bei 10 bis 11 richtigen: ***You're getting better and better!*** Und bei 12 richtigen haben wir einen ***new champion!***

Der Vergleich mit „je – desto"

Für diese Art des Vergleichs brauchst du den *comparative*, also **die erste Steigerungsstufe, und den bestimmten Artikel** *(the definite article).*

<u>Je</u> schneller, <u>desto</u> besser! → *<u>The</u>* ***faster,*** *<u>the</u>* ***better.***

<u>Je</u> länger ich darüber nachdenke, <u>desto</u> mehr Zweifel habe ich. →
<u>The</u> ***longer*** *I think about it, <u>the</u>* ***more*** *doubts [dauts;* = Zweifel*] I have.*

Versuchen wir eine einfache Übersetzungsübung aus dem Deutschen ins Englische. Es geht – natürlich – um „je" und „desto".

1. Je älter, desto klüger.
2. Je länger der Film, desto besser.
3. Je stärker der Gegner, desto spannender die Spiele. (Gegner = opponent; spannend = exciting)
4. Je größer der Garten, desto schwerer die Arbeit.
5. Je länger ich schlafe, desto müder bin ich am Morgen.
6. Je später du beginnst, desto schneller musst du arbeiten.
7. Je länger du wartest, desto schwieriger wird alles.
8. Je schneller wir fahren, desto früher sind wir dort. (früh = hier: soon)

„gefährliche Wörter"

Wir wenden uns jetzt einer besonderen Gruppe von Wörtern zu. Sie klingen sehr ähnlich, man schreibt sie sehr ähnlich, sie bedeuten auch etwas Ähnliches, aber: **Du darfst sie nicht verwechseln!**

die ***„ing"*-Gruppe** (wie etwas oder jemand ist)		die ***„ed"*–Gruppe** (wie man sich fühlt)	
*bor**ing***	langweil**ig**	*bor**ed***	gelangweil**t**
*interest**ing***	interess**ant**	*interest**ed***	interessier**t**
*surpris**ing***	überrasch**end**	*surpris**ed***	überrasch**t**
*terrify**ing***	erschreck**end**	*terrifi**ed***	erschreck**t**
*shock**ing***	schockier**end**	*shock**ed***	schockier**t**
*amaz**ing***	erstaun**lich**	*amaz**ed***	erstaun**t**
*excit**ing***	aufreg**end**	*excit**ed***	aufgereg**t**

Also: Wenn etwas **aufregend** ist, dann bist du selbst **aufgeregt**.
Wenn jemand **interessant** ist, dann bist du an ihm / ihr **interessiert**.

*If something is **exciting,** you are **excited.***
*If somebody is **interesting,** you are **interested** in him.*

TIPP Sage dir mehrere solche Sätze vor! *The more, the better!*

Welche Form stimmt, die mit *"ing"* oder die mit *"ed"*? Streiche das unpassende Wort durch!

example: It was surprising / surprised that we won the match.
Even our coach was surprising / surprised. →

It was surprising / ~~surprised~~ that we won the match.
Even our coach was ~~surprising~~ / surprised.

1. The film we saw last week was very boring / bored.
2. I was so exciting / excited when I met her for the first time.
3. "Animal Farm" is a very interesting / interested book; even my sister was surprising / surprised by it.
4. Who's making this terrifying / terrified noise? Stop it, please!
5. I'm selling my comics collection. Are you interesting / interested?
6. It was exciting / excited for us all to meet the big TV-star.
7. We were really shocking / shocked when we saw the accident.
8. It was the most shocking / shocked situation we had ever seen.
9. What an amazing / amazed story! Nobody will believe it!
10. Why are you looking so boring / bored? Don't you like the party?
11. Ms Perry was amazing / amazed that we had not forgotten her birthday.
12. Little children are sometimes terrifying / terrified when they wake up in the middle of the night.

3

Mach gleich weiter so und zeig, was du kannst!

1. I was boring / bored all day because I didn't know what to do.
2. My sister was terrifying / terrified when the cat scratched her.
3. Were you interesting / interested in what they said?
4. Yes, I was. They told us a lot of amazing / amazed things.
5. Edward had a most surprising / surprised idea.
6. The children were shocking / shocked about the war photos.
7. The most shocking / shocked picture was that of a dead baby.
8. Your report was interesting / interested and surprising / surprised.
9. The audience were much surprising / surprised about the report.
10. It was terrifying / terrified how he did his tricks on the trapeze.
11. The new CD was very interesting / interested.
12. I was surprising / surprised when you said the book was boring / bored.

How did you do? 14 bis 12 Punkte: ***Very interesting!*** 11 bis 9: ***Surprising!*** Weniger als 9: ***Shocking and terrifying!***

noch mehr Vergleiche

Zwei Vergleichsmöglichkeiten kennst du ja schon (eine mit dem *comparative,* eine mit dem *superlative*).

☆ *Susi ist* ***faster than / more beautiful than*** *all other girls.*
(schneller, schöner, . . . **als** . . .)

☆ *A Rolls Royce is one of the* ***most elegant*** *cars in the world.*
It is also one of the ***longest*** *cars.*
(der / die / das längste, eleganteste, . . . **überhaupt**)

Jetzt kommen **noch drei Vergleichsmöglichkeiten** dazu!

as . . . as

Damit vergleichst du **Gleiches mit Gleichem**: A ist **so wie** B.

*Tom is **as tall as** his brother.*	(nicht größer und nicht kleiner)
*Rafting is **as expensive as** canoeing.*	(ganz genauso teuer)
*One test is **as bad as** the other.*	(Die sind alle gleich mies!)

not as . . . as
not so . . . as

Damit vergleichst du Ungleiches miteinander: A ist **nicht so wie** B.

*Tom is **not as tall as** his dad.*	(Dad ist immer noch größer!)
*Rafting is **not so expensive as** flying.*	(Nur Fliegen ist teurer!)
*A maths test is **not as bad as** the rest.*	(Ein Mathe-Test nicht!)

Es ist übrigens **egal, ob du *"not as . . . as"* oder *"not so . . . as"*** sagst:
*One is **as good as** the other!*

a most . . .

Damit sagst du, dass A **etwas Besonderes, Unübertroffenes** ist. Das geht aber **nur bei** den Adjektiven, die mit ***more* und *most*** gesteigert werden!

Vorsicht! Nicht mit *the most . . .* **verwechseln!** Das bedeutet nämlich das größte, schönste, teuerste, . . . überhaupt!

„Das Boot" was ***a most exciting*** *film.*	(ein besonders spannender Film)
Tomorrow will be ***a most important*** *day.*	(ein ganz bedeutender Tag)
Last week I had ***a most awful*** *exam.*	(eine ganz schreckliche Prüfung)

67 Jetzt musst du gut mitdenken, sonst geht diese Übung daneben! Überlege dir bei jedem Satz, was gemeint ist, und setze dann die richtige Vergleichsform ein.

1. A mouse is (clever) . . . a cat, and that is why cats catch and eat mice.
2. Harry is (tall) . . . Fred, because Fred is older.
3. I saw David Copperfield doing (unusual) . . . trick on TV last night. (unusual = ungewöhnlich)
4. Oranges are much (sweet) . . . lemons.
5. I was late, but I tried to get there (fast) . . . I could.
6. I am sorry, but it's true. Joe is (strong) . . . you.
7. This tree is (tall) . . . that one over there. They are both 12 metres.
8. It's (cold) . . . yesterday: minus 10° yesterday, only minus 3° today!
9. Joe made a (terrible) . . . mistake in his driving test: he crashed into another car!
10. To me, biology is (important) . . . geography. They are both quite interesting, I think.

4 Du kannst dich *here and now* zur Höchstform steigern, wenn es um die Steigerung in allen ihren Formen geht. Setze also immer die passenden Formen des Adjektivs ein (und sonstige fehlende Wörter, wie z. B. *than*), und du wirst es nicht bereuen! *May the best win!*

❍ 1. My new bike was (cheap) . . . I thought. Now I even have some money left.

❍ 2. This was (interesting) . . . exercise. Let's do it again soon!

❍ 3. I don't like geography this year. It's much (boring) . . . last year.

❍❍ 4. Which of you can run (fast) . . . , Bill or Jeremy? – Jerry! He is (fast) . . . of our class.

❍❍ 5. I've read somewhere that Bill Gates of Microsoft is the (rich) . . . man in the world. – I don't think that's true. I've read that the Sultan of Brunei is even (rich) . . . Bill Gates.

❍❍ 6. We complained about the food, but it did not help. It got (bad) . . . and (bad) . . .

❍❍ 7. Look at Joan! She is two years (young) . . . Victoria, but she is (tall) . . . her. They are both 1.60 metres, I think.

❍❍ 8. Our team is not (strong) . . . last year. Let's hope the next season will be (good) . . .

❍ 9. Congratulations, Melanie! This was your (good) . . . game today.

❍ 10. On Saturday we had a (excellent) . . . dinner at the Shermans' house.

❍❍ 11. January is usually the (cold) . . . month of year where I live, but last winter February was much (cold) . . .

❍❍ 12. To me and my friends, football is as (boring/bored) . . . baseball, but we all think basketball is the (interesting) . . .

Not as simple as it looks, is it? Gar nicht so einfach! Aber 17 von 19 Punkten reichen für ein ***very good!*** Bei weniger als 7: ***The situation is getting more and more critical!***

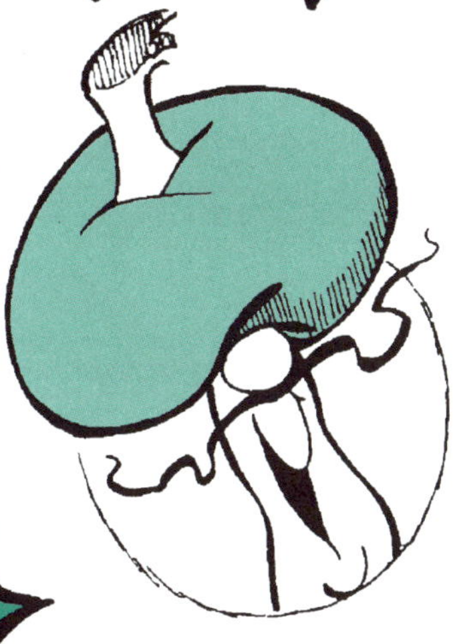

MUDRA FÜR DEN GESUNDEN WILLEN

Du hast keine Lust zu lernen?

Diese Lernunwilligkeit kannst du folgendermaßen abbauen:

Du legst den Zeigefinger in die Daumengrube und bringst Daumen und Mittelfingerkuppe zusammen.

Das Mudra kannst du mit beiden Händen gleichzeitig oder jeweils mit einer Hand halten. Immer dann, wenn du eine Hand gerade nicht brauchst, hältst du die Finger in der beschriebenen Stellung.

Hervorragend geeignet zum Hinhören im Unterricht, beim Schreiben und Nachdenken. Sogar während des Lesens kannst du es halten.

Dauer der Übung: mindestens 7 Minuten

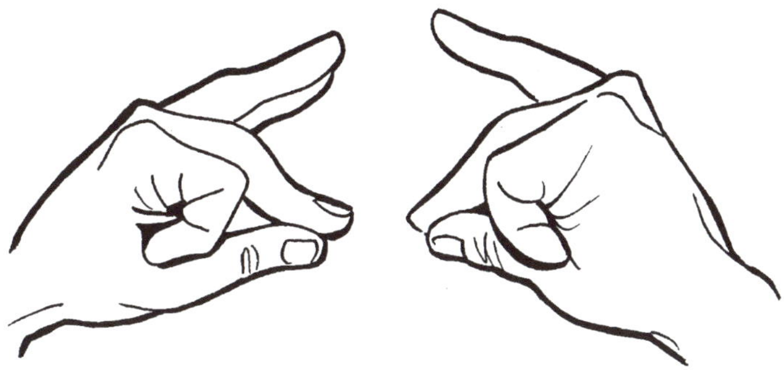

DAS FÜRWORT
THE PRONOUN

Das bezügliche Fürwort (the relative pronoun)

Die ***relative pronouns*** (die bezüglichen Fürwörter) sind alte Bekannte. Du weißt bereits, wie man

who, which, that, whose und ***whom***

anwendet. (Passende Informationen erhältst du auch in „Durchstarten in Englisch für die 6. Schulstufe", ab Seite 106.)

☆ ***who (that) – whose*** (im zweiten Fall) ***– who(m)*** (im „dritten" und „vierten Fall")

The girl who *sits beside me in class . . .*
The girl that *sits beside me in class . . .*
The man whose *house we can see from here . . .*
The woman who(m) *we'll visit tomorrow . . .*

☆ ***that / which – whose*** (im zweiten Fall)

The bridge that / which *leads across the river . . .*
The dog that / which *is playing over there . . .*
Animals whose lives *are in danger . . .*

☆ meist ***that***

The ***fastest*** *car* ***that*** *is built in Germany . . .*
The ***only*** *person* ***that*** *can help us . . .*

68

Das Gelernte kannst du jetzt gleich in die Tat umsetzen. Schreibe *who, which, that* oder *whose* an die richtigen Stellen.

1. I know lots of people . . . think only of themselves.
2. Roads . . . lead through the mountains can be dangerous in winter.
3. Are you the man . . . daughter was bitten by a dog?
4. A car . . . engine (= Motor) does not work isn't worth much.
5. Timothy was the only candidate . . . knew the answer.
6. The dark-haired woman . . . is talking to your mum is my Aunt Vera.
7. Those of you . . . want to go to the disco must ask their parents first.
8. My grandfather was the oldest man . . . climbed the Matterhorn.

Jetzt aber aufgepasst, denn weiter geht's mit den **„Neuheiten"** und **„Feinheiten"** der 7. Schulstufe!

1

Im modernen Englisch wird ***that* meist statt *which*** verwendet. (Wann und wo das nicht möglich ist, erfährst du in der 8. Schulstufe!)

Statt:

The bridge ***which*** *leads across the river . . .*

sagt und hört man eher:

The bridge ***that*** *leads across the river . . .*

69

Das kannst du jetzt gleich selbst üben. Suche die Sätze aus *exercise 68*, die mit *which* gebildet werden, und ersetze *which* durch *that.*
Hinweis: Es ist nur ein Satz!

70

Ein Satz macht aber keine Übung! Deshalb hast du noch einmal die Chance, dein Können unter Beweis zu stellen. Setze *who* (für Personen) und diesmal *that* (für Dinge und Tiere) ein.

1. The pictures . . . are hanging on the walls of our living room were painted by Charlie.
2. A waiter or a waitress is a person . . . serves food and drinks.
3. The person . . . spoke to me on the phone was very friendly.
4. The name of the horse . . . won the race was "Majestix".
5. "Dances with Wolves" is a book and a film . . . tells the story of a white man . . . lives with Indians.
6. Everybody . . . saw the show liked it.
7. Mum works in a shop . . . sells clothes.
8. Do you know the lady . . . has just left?

2

Die zweite „Feinheit": In **bestimmten Fällen braucht man überhaupt kein *relative pronoun*;** das heißt, man kann es einfach weglassen! Das gilt für *who, which, that* und *whom,* nicht aber für *whose.*

Wie soll man aber erkennen, wo man das *pronoun* braucht und wo nicht? Keine Angst, das geht recht einfach! Schau dir dazu die folgenden Beispiele an:

☆ *The girl / boy – **she / he** sits beside me in class – is very clever.*
*The girl / boy **who** sits beside me in class is very clever.*

*These are the children – **they** called the police after the accident.*
*These are the children **who** called the police after the accident.*

*The bridge – **it** leads across the river – is 500 years old.*
*The bridge **that (which)** leads across the river is 500 years old.*

*The flowers – **they** grow in your garden – are beautiful.*
*The flowers **that (which)** grow in your garden are beautiful.*

R

In diesen Sätzen steht **who** anstelle von **he / she / they**,
that (which) anstelle von **it / they**.

who / that (which) ist somit das **Subjekt** dieser Sätze. Wenn das der Fall ist, darf man *who / that / which* **nicht weglassen**!

TIPP

Das *relative pronoun* ist Subjekt, wenn danach ein Verb steht!

☆ *The friends – we invited **them** to the party – could not come.*
*The friends **who / whom** we invited to the party could not come.*

*The jeans – I bought **them** yesterday - are too small.*
*The jeans **that (which)** I bought yesterday are too small.*

*Did you like the castle? We visited **it** yesterday.*
*Did you like the castle **that / which** we visited yesterday?*

R

In diesen Sätzen steht ***who / whom*** anstelle von ***him / her / them,***
that (which) anstelle von ***it / them***.

who(m) / that / which ist somit das **Objekt** dieser Sätze (also der dritte oder vierte Fall). Wenn das der Fall ist, darf man *who / that / which* auch **weglassen**! Solche Sätze heißen ***contact clauses,*** weil der Relativsatz in direkten Kontakt mit dem Hauptsatz tritt (Symbol: •).

Die Mustersätze lauten daher im modernen Alltagsenglisch:

The friends • ***we*** *invited to the party could not come.*

The jeans • ***I*** *bought yesterday are too small.*

Did you like the castle • ***we*** *visited yesterday?*

TIPP

Das *relative pronoun* ist Objekt, wenn danach ein ***personal pronoun*** oder ein Name steht! → Du kannst es weglassen!

Zuletzt noch ein ganz wichtiger Tipp: ***whose*** darf man überhaupt **nie weglassen!**

71

Du sollst nun die richtigen *relative pronouns* dort **einsetzen,** wo sie hingehören, und sie dort **weglassen,** wo das möglich ist.

examples: I like films . . . show the life of animals. →
I like films that (which) show the life of animals.

- ☆ *that,* weil es um eine Sache geht;
- ☆ nicht weglassen, weil *that* statt des Subjekts steht *(They show the life of animals);*
- ☆ auf *that* folgt ein Zeitwort.

"Robinson Crusoe" is the best book . . . I know. →
"Robinson Crusoe" is the best book (that) I know.

- ☆ weglassen, weil das *relative pronoun* hier anstelle des Objekts stehen würde *(I know it);*
- ☆ auf das *relative pronoun* folgt ein *personal pronoun.*

1. The waiter . . . served us was very polite, and so we left him a big tip.
2. The book is about the man . . . invented the telephone. His name was Alexander Graham Bell.
3. The police caught the man . . . stole my car. I'll get it back soon.
4. Are you the mechanic? I am the man . . . car has broken down.
5. A dictionary is a book . . . tells you the meaning of words. I've got a big one at home. Have you got one, too?
6. The teacher . . . name I have forgotten died last week. He was quite old, I think.
7. Please bring me the bag . . . I put on the table. All my money is in it.
8. This is the last sentence . . . we'll do today. Then you can go out and play with your friends.
9. Do you remember the pretty girl . . . we saw at Timmy's party in summer? She is in my class now.
10. The cheapest hotel room . . . Uncle Fred could find was £ 25 per night.
11. The person . . . I like best in the world is my older brother Jack. He is just great.
12. The new houses . . . they are building in our village look very nice.

***Relative pronouns* leiten *relative clauses* ein** (das sind „Relativsätze"). Diese werden oft verwendet, um zwei Sätze zu einem zu verbinden. Diese **Satzverkürzung oder Satzverknüpfung** ist ein Zeichen von gutem Stil! Präge sie dir daher gut ein und wende sie auch an, vor allem beim Schreiben.

Der Relativsatz steht dabei immer **unmittelbar nach dem Bezugswort.** Übrigens: Du hast bei all den bisherigen Übungen solche *relative clauses* gebildet und angewendet, ohne dass es dir vielleicht bewusst war.

Sehen wir uns die Sache noch einmal im Detail an:

Statt *Where are **the posters**? **They** were hanging above your bed.*
gilt: *Where are **the posters that/which** were hanging above your bed?*

Statt: ***The cake*** *was excellent. We bought* ***it*** *this morning.*
gilt: ***The cake (that / which)*** *we bought this morning was very good.*

Solltest du jemals aufgefordert werden, eine Übung dieser Art zu machen – und das ist schon bei *exercise 72* der Fall – dann denke bitte daran:

Der Relativsatz folgt sofort auf das Bezugswort!!!

72

Make one sentence out of two, und zwar mit Hilfe von Relativsätzen *(relative clauses)*. Denke daran, dass

☆ der Relativsatz immer sofort nach dem Bezugswort steht;

☆ das *relative pronoun* in bestimmten Fällen wegfallen kann.

TIPP

Bei den ersten fünf Sätzen findest du das Bezugswort am Satzende. Bei den übrigen Sätzen steht es entweder am Satzanfang oder in der Satzmitte (dann musst du den Relativsatz an dieser Stelle „einbauen"!)

1. I want a computer. It can do all my homework for me.
2. These are the keys! I lost them yesterday.
3. What's the name of the woman? She won the car in the lottery.
4. From here you can see the mountain. We climbed it last weekend.
5. Is that the boy? His cat has disappeared. (= verschwinden)
6. The women were very helpful. They gave us food and drink.
7. The river is called the Thames. It flows through London.
8. The girl is my cousin from New Zealand. You met her last night.
9. The museums are fantastic. We're going to visit them in London.
10. The man is my neighbour. His car was stolen.

Hast du dich bei all diesen Übungen manchmal gefragt, warum es hier keine Beistriche gibt? Die Antwort darauf gibt es in der 8. Schulstufe!

1

Finde die beste Möglichkeit: Das passende *relative pronoun* einsetzen oder weglassen, *that's the question*!

❍ 1. Do you know the phone number of the man . . . repaired your car?
❍ 2. At Harrod's you can buy everything . . . you want.
❍ 3. Are you the gentleman . . . has called the police?
❍ 4. We stayed at a hotel . . . was listed in the "London Hotel Guide".
❍ 5. The man . . . Monica has married comes from South Africa.
❍ 6. Are you the lady . . . son was hurt in the accident?
❍ 7. The other day (= vor ein paar Tagen) I met some people . . . went to elementary school (= Volksschule) with me.
❍ 8. The letter . . . came yesterday was from Aunt Sylvia in London.
❍ 9. The letter . . . we received yesterday was from Aunt Sylvia in London. (to receive = erhalten)
❍ 10. A butcher is a person . . . makes and sells sausages.
❍ 11. The police tried to help the tourists . . . passports had been stolen.
❍ 12. Is there a shop near here . . . sells postcards and stamps?
❍ 13. My friends are the only people . . . listen to me when I need help.
❍ 14. This is the house . . . roof collapsed during the snowstorm. (to collapse = einstürzen)
❍ 15. Many of the places . . . we wanted to visit were closed, so we had to do something else.
❍ 16. Do you like the things . . . they showed us at Madame Tussaud's?

16, 15 or 14 correct answers? ***You're relatively good!*** *13 or less?* ***Try again!***

Die zweite „Flaggenübung“ handelt von der Satzverknüpfung! Du musst je zwei Sätze mit Hilfe von Relativsätzen zu einem einzigen Satz verkürzen. Dabei sollst du das *relative pronoun* weglassen, wenn das möglich ist.

❍ 1. Many tourists travel by Underground. They visit the sights of London.
❍ 2. Where is the cake? It was on the kitchen table.
❍ 3. Where is the cake? I left it on the kitchen table.
❍ 4. The fish tasted very good. We had it for dinner yesterday.
❍ 5. The vase cost a lot of money. You dropped it. (to drop = fallen lassen)
❍ 6. I liked the pictures. We saw them in the Tate Gallery.
❍ 7. All the pictures are now back at the National Gallery. They were stolen last year.
❍❍ 8. "Jungle Book" is a film. It tells the story of a boy. He was raised by the animals of the jungle. (to raise = aufziehen)
❍ 9. I think this is the boy. His dog won the first prize at the dog show.
❍ 10. This is the man! I wanted to see him yesterday.
❍ 11. We are looking for a shop. It sells souvenirs and films.
❍ 12. That boy is my best friend. You met him at the party.
❍ 13. I bought the jeans in Oxford Street. I'm wearing them now.
❍ 14. In many countries children cannot go to school. Their parents do not have enough money.
❍ 15. This is our new neighbour. I always forget her name.

Wieder gab es 16 Punkte zu erreichen. Hast du alles richtig? ***Congratulations!***
Auch bei 15 oder 14 richtigen Lösungen kannst du stolz auf dich sein. Bei 13 oder weniger „Treffern“ schau dir die Sache lieber noch einmal an!

Das rückbezügliche Fürwort

Du hast sicher schon – ohne dass es dir vielleicht aufgefallen ist – die englischen ***reflexive pronouns*** kennen gelernt.

*I sometimes talk to **myself** in my sleep.*

*What's the matter with Peter? – He cut **himself** with his knife.*

*We often ask **ourselves** why we did not win the match.*

A

singular			***plural***		
I	*often talk to*	***myself.***	***We***	*often talk to*	***ourselves**.*
You	*often talk to*	***yourself.***	***You***	*often talk to*	***yourselves.***
He	*often talks to*	***himself**.*			
She	*often talks to*	***herself.***	***They***	*often talk to*	***themselves.***
*(**It***	*often talks to*	***itself**.)*			

!

Auf drei Dinge musst du besonders achten:

- ☆ Du sagst ***–self,*** wenn du von **einer Person** sprichst, du sagst ***–selves,*** wenn du von **mehreren Personen** sprichst.
- ☆ Du sagst daher ***yourself*** in der Einzahl und ***yourselves*** in der Mehrzahl.
- ☆ Du sagst ***himself*** und ***themselves*** und nicht *hisself* und *theirselves.*

Du verwendest das ***reflexive pronoun*** in folgenden Situationen:

1 Wenn es auf Deutsch heißt:

ich . . . mir / mich, du . . . dir / dich, er . . . sich,
wir . . . uns, ihr . . . euch oder **sie . . . sich**

My grandfather is a clever man. ***He*** *taught* ***himself*** *to read.*
Mein Opa ist ein kluger Mann. **Er** brachte **sich** das Lesen bei.

Be careful, children, or ***you*** *will hurt* ***yourselves.***
Seid vorsichtig, Kinder, oder **ihr** werdet **euch** verletzen.

This machine *will destroy* (= zerstören) ***itself*** *in ten seconds.*
Diese Maschine **(sie)** wird **sich** in zehn Sekunden zerstören.

73 Setze in den folgenden Sätzen die passenden *reflexive pronouns* ein.
Achte dabei besonders auf *singular (-self)* und *plural (-selves).*

1. Susi often looks at . . . in the mirror (= Spiegel).
2. Rumpelstiltskin was sooooo angry that he threw . . . on the ground.
3. Your car can't repair . . . ! You must take it to a mechanic.
4. My friends enjoyed . . . very much at my birthday party.
5. Boys, don't hurt . . . with those swords!
6. Tom, control . . . ! You can't shout here!
7. If I were a magician, I would turn . . . into a bird.
8. Don't worry, mum. We can look after . . . when you are away.
   (to look after = aufpassen)

Das ist **falsch,**	aber das ist **richtig**!
I *often make* ~~***me***~~ *a cheese roll.*	***I*** *often make* ***myself*** *a cheese roll.*
We *enjoyed* ~~***us***~~ *very much in our holidays.*	***We*** *enjoyed* ***ourselves*** *very much in our holidays.*
Charlie is an egoist. ***He*** *thinks only of* ~~***him***~~*.*	*Charlie is an egoist* ***He*** *thinks only of* ***himself****.*

2 Wenn man sagen will, dass jemand etwas **selbst** gemacht hat; diese Wörter heißen daher auch ***"self"-pronouns***.

I'm sorry I can't help you, Jane. ***You*** *have to do it* ***yourself****.*
Tut mir Leid, Jane. **Du** musst es **selbst** tun.

Who helped you find your watch? – Nobody. ***I*** *found it* ***myself****.*
Wer hat . . . geholfen? – Niemand. **Ich** habe sie **selbst** gefunden.

Who has made those dresses? – ***We*** *made them* ***ourselves****!*
Wer hat . . . gemacht? – **Wir** haben sie **selbst** gemacht.

74 Setze wieder die passenden *"self"-pronouns* ein, diesmal in der Bedeutung von „selbst".

1. We don't need a mechanic. We can repair the car . . . .
2. Don't ask your dad for help, Joe. You must do your homework . . . .
3. My mother was in Berlin last week, so I had to make breakfast . . . .
4. Uncle Albert is a lazy man. He never washes his car . . . .
5. The film was about a robot that was so perfect that it could program . . . .

6. Are you sure that Conrad is ill? – Yes, I am. His mother said so . . . .
7. Kevin, Sally and James, did you really write these songs . . .? – Yes, we did. Do you like them?
8. Mr and Mrs Novak's new house is fantastic, isn't it? – Yes, it is. Did you know that they planned it . . .?

3 Manchmal wird das *reflexive pronoun* verwendet, um **eine Person oder ein Ding besonders hervorzuheben.**

Mr Wilson himself *allowed us to play in his garden.*
Er selbst hat es uns erlaubt. (Nicht etwa seine Frau oder sein Sohn!)

What do you think of the Thompsons' new house? – Well, ***the house itself*** *is fantastic, but the garden is too small, I think.*
(**Das Haus selbst** ist in Ordnung. Aber der Garten . . . ?)

75

Setze das passende *"self"-pronoun* ein, das die Person oder den Gegenstand besonders betont.

1. I'm sure you have heard about the fire in our street because I . . . told you about it.
2. The film . . . wasn't so good, but everybody liked the party later.
3. Lord Melville . . . showed us the castle and the garden. He is a very friendly old man.
4. Do you think we should really begin the match in this terrible weather? – Well, I'm sure the players . . . want to play.
5. Look, what a lovely letter! Caroline . . . has invited us to her birthday party. Are you going?
6. It's not the battery and it's not the starter. Something is wrong with the engine . . . (engine = Motor)

Es gibt Zeitwörter, die im Deutschen ein rückbezügliches Fürwort verlangen, im Englischen aber nicht!

A Diese Zeitwörter sind natürlich eine ständig sprudelnde Fehlerquelle. Du solltest dir daher die wichtigsten „Revoluzzer" gut einprägen!

to afford

Wir können **uns** kein neues Auto leisten.
We cannot afford *a new car.*
(nicht: *We cannot afford ourselves a new car.*)

to feel (+adjective)

Ich fühle **mich** heute sehr gut.
I feel *very good today.*

to hurry

Du musst **dich** beeilen, Tom.
You *must* ***hurry,*** *Tom.*

to meet

Sie trafen **sich** jeden Tag nach der Schule.
They met *after school every day.*

to remember

Kim kann **sich** nicht an ihre Großmutter erinnern.
Kim cannot remember *her grandmother.*

to worry

Eltern machen **sich** oft Sorgen um ihre Kinder.
Parents often worry *about their children.*

Auch ***to dress*** und ***to wash*** (sich anziehen oder ankleiden, sich waschen) gehören in diese Gruppe.

76 *Reflexive pronouns (myself, yourself, . . .) or not?* Du entscheidest! Setze die Fürwörter dort ein, wo sie hingehören; mache ein **✗**, wenn kein Fürwort hergehört. Beachte die „Revoluzzer"!

example: After I get up, I wash . . . and dress . . . →
After I get up, I wash ✗ and dress ✗.

1. When Susi was skiing last weekend, she fell and hurt . . .
2. Did you make this dress . . . , Monica? You must be very proud of . . .
3. I'm sure I have seen you before, but I cannot remember . . . where and when.
4. My dad plays the drums in a rock band. They meet . . . every Friday to practise new songs.
5. Here is the key to the house, children. You can let . . . in when you come home from the cinema.
6. Patricia has gone to bed. She does not feel . . . well tonight.
7. We have to use our old skis again this year because we cannot afford . . . new ones.
8. Don't be sad about the bad mark. Look at Betty! She never worries . . . about bad marks.

4 Keinesfalls darf man die *"self"-pronouns* mit **each other** oder **one another** verwechseln. Schau dir die folgenden Beispiele an, und du wirst den Unterschied leicht erkennen.

***Mac and Charlie** looked at **themselves** in the mirror and had a good laugh.*

***Mac and Charlie** looked at **each other (one another)** and had a good laugh.*

77 *"self"-pronoun or each other / one another?* Du entscheidest!

1. I met Jean yesterday afternoon and we talked to . . . for a long time.
2. You don't have to pay for us, Uncle Philip. We can pay for . . .
3. Our guests (= Gäste) did not speak English and we did not speak German. So we had to talk to . . . in French.
4. Did you enjoy . . . , girls? – Yes, Mr Wright. It was great.
5. Laura is a photographer, but she hasn't got any photos of . . .
6. Maxwell and Charlie are good friends, but they do not always understand . . . very well.

5 Zu guter Letzt noch ein Hinweis auf die Verbindung ***by + "self" – pronoun*** *(by myself, by himself, by yourselves, . . .).* Sie bedeutet soviel wie **allein / alleine** *(in English: **alone**).*

*After a hard day's work **I** like to be **by myself**.*
Nach . . . bin **ich** gerne **allein**.

*Did **you** build these models **by yourself**? – Yes, I did!*
Hast **du** . . . **alleine** gebaut?

*When I saw Andrew yesterday, **he** was sitting in a café **by himself**.*
. . . saß **er allein** in einem Café.

***Young children** are not allowed to stay out **by themselves** at night.*
Sie . . . dürfen nach 22 Uhr nicht **alleine** weggehen.

78 Setze wieder das passende *reflexive pronoun* ein, diesmal mit *by*.

1. Nobody wants to help me water the flowers, so I must do it . . .
2. Harry and Sally wrote these stories . . . They are very clever, aren't they?
3. My moped didn't start . . . , so I had to ask my friends to push me.
4. Next summer my brother and I will go to Great Britain . . . , without our parents. We hope it will be fun.
5. My grandma lives in a big old house all . . . , but she doesn't like it.
6. Ted did you programme your computer . . . or did anybody help you?

Du kannst dir wieder Lorbeeren verdienen. Setze die passenden *"self"-pronouns* ein!
(Achte auf die „Ausnahmen": In drei Fällen musst du *by + reflexive pronoun* einsetzen; in drei Fällen darfst du kein *reflexive pronoun* verwenden!)

❍ 1. Frank, have you never asked . . . why your grades aren't better? – I know why they are so bad. It's because I don't study enough. (grades = Schulnoten)
❍ 2. Why are you so sure that the film starts at 8:15? – I called the cinema and they told me so . . .
❍ 3. I know where Joe and Norma live, but I can't remember . . . the name of the street.
❍ 4. The noise in the classroom made Mrs Brown so angry that she could not control . . . any longer. She banged her books on the desk and began to shout at us.
❍ 5. How did you like the Tower of London? – Well, The Crown Jewels and the armours (= Rüstungen) were fantastic, but the building . . . was a disappointment (= Enttäuschung).
❍ 6. Dad makes excellent cakes. He always bakes them . . . He says he will show me how to do it one day.
❍ 7. Mum, do you really have to go away for a week? We don't want to stay . . . so long!
❍ 8. What a silly, silly mistake! I'm so angry I could kick . . .
❍ 9. Do you make these blouses . . . , girls? – Yes, we do, but Mrs Lamb helps us with them.
❍ 10. My dad gets up early so that he doesn't have to hurry . . .
❍ 11. Look, you broke my ruler. Next time you need one, you can buy one . . . ! I'm not going to lend you mine again.
❍ 12. What do you think of England after your holiday there? – It's a great country with lots of interesting things to do. We enjoyed . . . very much while we were there.
❍ 13. How is Peter? Is he still in bed? – He is better, but he still feels . . . weak. I think he won't go to school again this week.
❍ 14. After a difficult maths test or before an important tennis match I like to be . . .

Hast du alle 14 richtig? ***You can be proud of yourself.*** Wenn du eine oder mehrere Aufgaben falsch gelöst hast, musst du noch üben, denn das *reflexive pronoun* ist eine recht einfache Sache.

NILPFERD

Du kannst dich nicht mehr konzentrieren?
Du sitzt schon viel zu lange bei deinen Hausaufgaben?

Tanke wieder Energie:
Du stehst, die Beine sind hüftbreit auseinander, die Füße zeigen gerade nach vorne. Die Knie sind gebeugt und leicht federnd. Du schwingst nun die gestreckten Arme abwechselnd nach vorne und hinten.
Achte darauf, dass der Arm vorne und der Arm rückwärts mit den Schultern eine Linie bilden.

Wiederholung der Übung:
50-mal mit jedem
Arm nach vorne

STORIES

Das Kapitel ***stories*** will dir helfen, eine ganz wichtige Fertigkeit in Englisch zu entwickeln: nämlich einen Gedanken, einen Text zu erfassen und auf verschiedene Weise wiederzugeben.

Auch dein Leseverständnis soll gefördert werden, damit du eine englische Geschichte und später einmal auch eine englische Zeitung lesen kannst, ohne gleich die Flinte ins Korn zu werfen.

Von alleine geht das aber nicht, und deshalb findest du im Anschluss an jede Geschichte kurze Übungen und Arbeitsaufgaben. Sie sind zum Teil schon anspruchsvoller als in den früheren Bänden von „Durchstarten in Englisch", aber du hast ja auch schon zwei volle Lernjahre hinter dir!

Folgende Arbeitsaufgaben kommen vor, wenn auch nicht immer alle bei jeder *story*:

1. *read the story* (Lesen)
2. *make sentences* (Sätze bilden)
3. *fill in* (Wörter einfügen)
4. *finish sentences* (Sätze weiterführen)
5. *right or wrong* (Richtig oder falsch)
6. *answer questions* (Fragen beantworten)
7. *why-questions* (Warum-Fragen)
8. *retell the story* (Nacherzählen)

Noch ein Tipp fürs Lesen:
Die Verwendung des Wörterbuches *(dictionary)* ist jetzt sinnvoller denn je. Schlage aber nicht sofort jedes Wort nach, das du nicht verstehst, sondern versuche zunächst, seinen Sinn aus dem Zusammenhang heraus zu erraten.

The Magic Bike

1 Read the story.

Lies dir die Geschichte einmal durch, ohne eine Pause einzulegen. Wenn du ein Wort nicht verstehst, lies zunächst weiter. Wenn du wirklich nicht dahinterkommst, was es bedeutet, kannst du in deinem Wörterbuch ***(dictionary)*** nachsehen.

Once there was an old man who sold second-hand things. He had a shop in one of the side streets in the centre of our little town. It wasn't a real shop, it was only a big room at the front of the house, and when you walked in, you couldn't see anybody. There was no shop assistant, and there was no friendly lady waiting to take your money. The sound of the old brass (= Messing) *bell over the entrance door made such a noise that the second-hand dealer knew somebody had come in. But then he did not smile and ask you what you wanted. He just walked round in the shop and didn't look at you. The shop was full of all kinds of old junk* (= Plunder), *things people normally throw away. And there were also some old bikes.*
One day a big, black car stopped right in front of the house. It was a new car and it looked clean and neat (= gepflegt). *A schoolgirl and a very elegant woman got out and together they entered the shop. The woman looked like a model in a fashion magazine* (= Modezeitschrift), *and the girl looked like the star of a TV-show. She was wearing a light-blue dress and white shoes and she behaved like a grown-up. The bell rang loudly when they opened the door, and this time the old man looked up at his customers* (= Kunden). *"My little princess would like to have an extraordinary bike", the woman announced* (= verkündete), *"A bike which the young generation would call 'cool', you understand?"*
The old man nodded (= nickte) *and walked over to a group of three rusty old bikes. "How extraordinary!" the lady said, and the girl asked in childish voice, "Can one paint the bikes pink? Pink is my favourite colour." The old man explained that the rust and the old paint had to be removed* (= entfernt) *before painting, and that would cost more money than the old bike itself. "No, that's too complicated!" the woman said, and, disappointed* (= enttäuscht), *the two of them left the shop and drove off in their big car.*

A little later a tall schoolboy and his elder brother came into the shop. They had very short hair and they wore big black jackets, trousers that were too big, and Dr Martens. Both had earphones round their heads, and you could hear the sound of heavy-metal music. "Hey, old man!" they shouted. "What about your bikes?" But when they heard about the work that had to be done to make the bikes look "cool" and "heavy", they left again, slamming the door behind them.

Perhaps you will ask how I came to know all these things. Well, I was looking for a bike myself in those days. My old bike had become far too small for me, and in fact, I had given it to Lucy, my little sister. My parents could not give me the money for a new bike, and so I had to use my own money. But I had only £ 20. So I took the bus to town every day to look for a cheap bike, a second-hand one, and on one of my searches (= Suche) I had come to the old man's shop. There I had seen and heard the woman and the girl and the two brothers.

Just before 6 o'clock that evening I entered the shop. The bell rang and the old man appeared. I knew what I wanted and so I went straight to one of the bikes. "You are lucky", the old man said. "It's a magic bike." "I'm nearly thirteen", I answered. "I know that there are no magic bikes." "This is one", said the man, who wanted to sell the bike. "But you must not wash it and you must not paint it, because that would take the magic away."

Magic or no magic, it was the bike for me. It cost only £ 10, so I had enough money to buy a comfortable saddle and some of the things you need to keep the police off your back (= sich die Polizei fernhalten).

When I got it home I looked it over carefully, and right under the saddle there was the word "MAGIC". A bit covered with dirt and rust, but it said "MAGIC". I told my parents that I was not supposed to clean or paint the bike, and mum said, "Then it's the right bike for you!"

And believe it or not, the bike is magic. On other bikes things get loose (= lose, locker) all the time, but on mine everything is tight and straight. And some strange things have happened. The lights usually don't work, so one evening, while I was riding home late, I was worried about the police because that night the lights didn't work again. Do you know what happened? After half a mile, just before I came to a roundabout (= Kreisverkehr), the front light went on!

Then, when we had a school outing on bikes, all the other kids had punctures (= Reifenpanne) along the way, but I had no problems. I rode over sharp rocks and pieces of broken glass, too, but my tyres didn't lose any air all day.

And once, when I went to the supermarket, I left my bike right outside the front door and not in the bike stand, because I didn't want to walk that far. When I came out again, my bike was gone! Of course I looked for it everywhere, but I couldn't find it. I was very sad and angry. But in the evening it was lying on the lawn in front of our house! It had come home by itself.
As I said – it's just the bike for me! It's a magic bike!

2 Fill in.

1 In our little town there was . . . things.
2 It wasn't a real . . . it was only . . . and when you walked in you . . .
3 The sound of . . . that the second-hand . . . in.
4 The shop was full . . . , things . . . away.
5 The car was new . . .
6 "My little princess . . . a bike which . . ."
7 The old man explained . . . had to be . . . and that would . . . itself.
8 Both had . . . round their heads, and you . . . music.
9 But when they heard . . . "cool" and "heavy" they . . .
10 So I took . . . to look for . . . , and on one of . . .
11 I knew what I . . . bikes.
12 "But you must not . . . or paint it because . . ."
13 It cost only . . . , so I had . . . saddle . . . you need . . . off your back.
14 The lights usually . . . while I was riding . . . work again.
15 And once . . . right outside the front door . . . walk that far.

3 Finish sentences.

1 It wasn't a real . . .
2 There was no shop assistant . . .
3 The sound of . . .
4 "My little princess . . ."
5 The old man explained that . . .
6 They had very short . . .
7 I told my parents that . . .
8 On other bikes things get loose . . .
9 When we had a school outing on bikes . . .

4 True or false?

1 There were a shop assistant and a lady at the cash desk (= Kassa).
2 The sound of the brass bell made a lot of noise.
3 The girl wore black shoes.
4 The old man explained that he would paint the bike pink if they bought it.
5 When the two boys heard about the work they left the shop.
6 "You must wash and clean the bike, but don't remove the paint", the old man said.
7 I bought the bike with my own money.
8 The bike cost 20 pounds.
9 I didn't put the bike in the bike stand when I went into the supermarket.

Hast du alle falschen Aussagen gefunden? Es waren diesmal fünf.

5 Answer questions.

1 Where was the old man's shop?
2 What did the woman look like?
3 What did the two brothers wear?
4 What made a loud noise when someone entered the shop?
5 How many bikes were there in the shop?
6 What did the bikes look like?
7 Who got the boy's old bike?
8 What happened to the other kids on the school outing?
9 Where did the boy find his bike at last?

6 Why-questions.

1 Why did the boy know what was going on round the shop?
2 Why did the lady and the boys not buy the bike?
3 Why didn't the boy's parents buy him a new bike?
4 Why was the boy not supposed to wash or clean the bike?
5 Why did he put his bike not in the bike stand?
6 Why did the boy "know" in the end that his bike was really magic?

7 Retell the Story.

Once there was an old man who . . . . He had a shop . . . . It wasn't a real . . . and when you walked in . . . . The sound of the bell . . . . The shop was full of . . . .
One day a girl . . . . The woman looked like . . . . And the girl looked . . . . "My little princess . . . ." But the old man said, "If . . . ."
The two schoolboys . . . . They both had . . . and they had earphones . . . . When they heard . . . slamming the door . . . .
I was looking for . . . . My old bike . . . my little sister. My parents could not . . . . £ 20. So I . . . .
Just before 6 o'clock . . . . I knew what I wanted so . . . . "You are lucky", the man said. ". . . ." "I am thirteen", I said. "I . . . ."
It cost only . . . so I had enough money to . . . . When I got it home . . . . It was a bit covered . . . . Mum said, "Then it's . . . !"
The bike is magic. On other bikes . . . . One evening, while I . . . . When we had a school outing . . . . I rode over . . . but . . . .
Once I went to a supermarket and . . . . Of course I looked . . . . In the evening . . . . It is a . . . .

The Christmas Present

1 Read the story.

Lies dir die Geschichte einmal durch, ohne eine Pause einzulegen. Wenn du ein Wort nicht verstehst, lies zunächst weiter. Wenn du wirklich nicht dahinterkommst, was es bedeutet, kannst du in deinem Wörterbuch ***(dictionary)*** nachsehen.

Children are not the only ones who like Christmas presents. Everybody likes them. And most people think when they get a Christmas present it is because somebody loves them. Sometimes this is true, and sometimes it is not only true, but also something else.
Pamela was a thirteen-year-old girl. She lived in Germany – in Berlin, to be more exact. Berlin is a wonderful city with old traditions, and it has had to live with the consequences (= Folgen) *of the Second World War. That was long ago. Pamela's mother was born after the war, but he grandparents had lived through it. Most girls Pamela's age know little about the war. Perhaps they know the dates, but not much more. Berlin suffered* (= leiden) *very much during the war and especially in the years after the war. Pamela knew a lot about that war. She had heard about the problems between Germans and Jews, between Germans and the French, between Germans and almost everybody else. But Pamela had no problems, of course. As I said before, that was a long time ago.*
When Pamela had a birthday party, or when one of her friends had a birthday party, she invited Li Chin-Chi, the son of the owner of the Chinese restaurant at the corner, and Paola, the pizzaman's daughter, and Mirko, the son of her father's workmate (= Arbeitskollege), *and everybody invited Magdi, the doctor's son, because it was great fun when he imitated TV stars. And, of course, everybody invited most of the class.*
And then one day in August, out of the blue (= aus heiterem Himmel), *Pamela met Abdi. Abdi was fifteen, and he was wonderful. He could talk, he could listen, he knew the answers to her problems, he was funny, he was nice, he was as good as gold. And he looked good, too! Whenever Pamela looked at him she felt her heart beat faster. And she felt that her belly* (= Bauch) *was full of butterflies.*

Abdi's real name was Abdullah, of course, and he would never touch a sandwich with sausage or meat in it. He would never touch a hotdog. But he liked Coke and Pepsi, chips, Heavy Metal, and his family. And when he met Pamela, he started liking her, too. The girl didn't say much about Abdi at home. Only her grandmother knew about him. Pamela's mum and dad were at work all day. Her mother was a cashier (= Kassierin) *in a big department store. She usually came home at four. Her dad always tried to make some extra money by doing extra work, and he usually came home after seven. So Pamela's parents did not really know what their daughter was doing in the afternoons.*

Abdi was a boy that didn't show off (= angeben). *He never wanted to impress* (= beeindrucken) *other people. He did not smoke the way other boys did to show how cool they were. He did not watch late-night movies, and, most unusual of all, he did not talk back to his parents. He even said that he liked them. When his dad asked him to do this or that, Abdi got up and did it. He never tried to be someone else, and he enjoyed life.*

All that was new to Pamela, because most of the boys she knew were not like that. With Abdi she could have a lot of fun: Abdi could juggle (= jonglieren) *three marbles at the same time, for example. It was amazing, but he threw them up in the air and caught them again. Two marbles were always in the air. Pamela tried it too, but it wouldn't work for her.*

Abdi did not live near Pamela. When they wanted to see each other, they had to take three different underground lines, and then there was still a walk of four blocks.

One day Pamela had come to Abdi's place. She said hello to Abdi's father and his brothers and sisters, and then they went for a walk. It was a sunny afternoon, and at around five o'clock they felt hungry. The two children didn't have to look long before they found a fast-food restaurant, and they went in. Pamela felt like a grown-up; her mother had given her some money when she had asked her for it, so there was no problem about paying for the food. But Abdi seemed to feel uneasy. There was a menu on the table and Pamela started to read it. The girl was all happiness. She was making funny faces and noises while she was reading the list of food and drinks, and then she asked Abdi if he wanted a special dish called "Chicken King". Abdi didn't say a word. Pamela said, "It's under ‚Chicken', page four, number 405." Abdi still said nothing. Now Pamela looked at him. There was a look in Abdi's face that Pamela had never seen before. His eyes went up and down and around the menu, but he did not really see what the menu said. Pamela watched him in asthonishment. He wouldn't look that way unless . . . (= wenn nicht . . .).

Suddenly Pamela wanted to say something but she found no words. The only words she could think of were "Why?" and "How?". But she could not speak. She noticed that Abdi could not speak either. They had talked about so many things, but never about that. They ordered a glass of orange juice each and drank in silence. Then they left the restaurant.
Outside, Abdi simply said, like a grown-up, "I can't read, Pamela. And I can't write." "Didn't you go to school?" Pamela asked. "Oh yes, I did", Abdi answered, "but there were more important things to do. I could read the lessons, of course, because I knew them by heart. But now it's all gone." "Don't you need to read sometimes? I mean, the TV-programme or something?" Pamela asked in surprise. "Not really", Abdi said. "Most of the things you know without reading or writing." They walked on in silence. "Would you want to learn it?" Pamela asked. "No, I don't want to go to school anymore." Abdi said. "I'm fifteen, and they would all laugh at me." "I could teach you", Pamela said. "Are you good at reading and writing?" Abdi wanted to know, but Pamela did not know what to say. "I promise I won't laugh", she said. "I would like to teach you. Really!"
When Pamela came home that day, her mother wondered why she was still so hungry. "Didn't you have anything to eat?" she asked, but Pamela did not want to talk about it.
Next day Pamela went to her grandmother. "Do you still have those old schoolbooks you had when you went to school?" she asked. Granny went into her bedroom and opened an old cardboard box (= Pappschachtel). *There were some old books and some old, grey notebooks. And there was also the reader* (= Lesebuch) *from Granny's first year at school. "1B", it said on the cover, in a child's hand* (= Handschrift). *Pamela opened the book. The first letter was "I". A picture showed some children standing around an appletree. They all wanted to have an apple and so they shouted, "I". And the whole book was like this. Each letter had a little story to make it easier to learn. Pamela looked through the book carefully. Then she looked through her grandmother's notebooks. Then she said, "I'll bring them back, I promise!"*
Grandmothers never say no to their grandchildren, and so Pamela went off with the books and three notebooks. At home she did not say much. The following days and weeks she spent in her room and did not even watch TV much. In late November she often left the house to study for a test, she said. And then, in December, her grandmother asked her if she still needed her old books. She also wanted to know what Pamela wanted for Christmas. Pamela's wish had always been a CDplayer, and that is what she told Granny now.

Two days before Christmas Pamela had finished all her shopping. She had a keyring for her dad's car keys, because the old one was broken, and then she had a video-tape for mum – "Gone with the Wind", mum's favourite film – and a digital alarm clock for Granny. Her old one was making so much noise in the night, she had once said. And then she had a beautiful blue pen for Abdi.
At Christmas they were all together, mum, dad, Granny, and Pamela. Pamela had got a fantastic CDplayer, a pair of Levi's, a new T-shirt, and sheets for her bed with cats on them. Everything was wonderful. Pamela looked at her Christmas presents and then she put her hand in one pocket. There she could feel a sheet of paper from a notebook. It was still there. The letter! The most wonderful letter in the world. The most wonderful Christmas present in the world. Secretly, so that nobody could see, she opened it and read it again. There, written in an insecure (hier: ungeübt) *hand, were the words "FRÖLICHE WEINACHTN UND EIN GLÜKLICHES NEUES JAHR. ABDI." Then Pamela went to her family, sat down on Granny's knees and said, "I love you all very much. And I like my Christmas presents." They were all happy, and Pamela was the happiest of them all. But she did not say a word to the others about why she was so happy!*

2 Make sentences.

Bilde Sätze mit den folgenden Wörtern aus der Geschichte (aber nicht die Sätze aus der Geschichte abschreiben!)

1 consequences
2 to invite
3 to feel
4 to enjoy
5 uneasy
6 to notice
7 to promise
8 insecure

3 Finish sentences.

1 Pamela's mother was born . . . but her grandparents . . .
2 When Pamela had a birthday party, . . .
3 Abdi would never . . . but most unusual of all, . . .
4 When Pamela asked Abdi if he wanted a . . .
5 Pamela wanted to say something but . . .
6 Next day Pamela went to her grandmother and . . .
7 The first letter was "I". A picture showed . . .
8 Pamela had finished all her shopping. She had . . .

4 Answer questions.

1 What do you know about Pamela's parents and grandparents?
2 a) What would Abdi never do?
b) What did Pamela like about Abdi?
3 Why did Pamela feel like a grown-up in the fast-food restaurant?
4 a) Why did Pamela watch Abdi in astonishment?
b) Why did they only drink a glass of juice there?
5 Why did Abdi not want to go to school again?
6 Why was it not necessary for Abdi to read or write?
7 a) Why did Pamela go to her grandmother?
b) What did Pamela promise her?
8 Why did her parents not know what she was doing all day long?
9 Describe Granny's reader.
10 What did Pamela get for Christmas and what did she buy?
11 a) What was there in Pamela's pocket and how did she feel?
b) Why did Pamela not tell anybody about her feelings?

5 Retell the story.

Die Nacherzählung solltest du erst versuchen, wenn du alle anderen Übungen bewältigt hast. Vergleiche dann dein Ergebnis mit der Textvorlage. Eine ganz genaue Kontrolle *deiner* Geschichte nimmt vielleicht deine Lehrerin oder dein Lehrer vor, wenn du sie / ihn darum bittest. Um festzustellen, ob *dein* Englisch stimmt, braucht sie / er die Originalgeschichte ja nicht, sondern nur deine Arbeit.

MUDRA
ZUM GEHIRNEINSCHALTEN

Dir fehlt die zündende Idee?
Du hast Angst, dass dir bei der Prüfung nichts mehr einfällt?
Dir fehlt die Motivation zum Lernen?

Schalte dein Gehirn wieder ein:
Du legst die Daumenkuppen auf Ring- und Kleinfingernagel.
Halte diese Stellung mit beiden Händen gleichzeitig.
Das Mudra solltest du 6-mal täglich machen. Natürlich auch dann, wenn du dein Gehirn dringendst brauchst; vor einer Prüfung zum Beispiel.

Dauer der Übung:
mindestens 4 Minuten

ARBEITEN MIT DEM WÖRTERBUCH

WORKING WITH THE DICTIONARY

Im 3. Lernjahr solltest du den Umgang mit dem Wörterbuch lernen, dem ***dictionary***.

Bis zum Vorjahr hat wahrscheinlich deine Lehrerin oder dein Lehrer die meisten der neuen englischen Wörter („Vokabeln") und deren Bedeutung an die Tafel geschrieben, aber ab jetzt solltest du selbst herausfinden, was ein englisches Wort oder ein Ausdruck auf Deutsch bedeutet und umgekehrt. Damit du dein Wörterbuch auch richtig benutzen kannst, sollst du ein wenig über dieses nützliche Buch erfahren.

Zunächst Grundsätzliches:

Es gibt Wörterbücher in vielen Größen und für viele Zwecke. Die „Größe" eines Wörterbuches wird angegeben in der Anzahl seiner **Stichwörter**; das sind die Wörter, die du im Wörterbuch nachschlagen kannst. Schulwörterbücher haben für gewöhnlich einen Umfang von etwa 35.000 bis 40.000 Stichwörtern.

Daneben gibt es auch das „Große Schulwörterbuch". Es umfasst bereits etwa 120.000 bis 130.000 Stichwörter. Wir wollen uns aber hier mit dem kleineren beschäftigen, weil es vorläufig für dich ausreicht. Außerdem ist das „Große" genauso aufgebaut.

Also, wenn du so ein Wörterbuch besitzt, dann nimm es einmal zur Hand und blättere eine Seite nach der anderen auf. Auf einer der ersten Seiten kannst du lesen, welcher **Verlag** das Wörterbuch hergestellt hat. Anschließend findest du das **Inhaltsverzeichnis**. (Das Inhaltsverzeichnis kann auch am Ende des Buches stehen.) Wenn du es durchliest, wirst du sehen, dass ein Wörterbuch nicht nur ein Wörterverzeichnis enthält, sondern viele andere nützliche Dinge.

Das **Vorwort** wird dich kaum interessieren, und du kannst es auch getrost überblättern. Meist gibt es Auskunft darüber, wie das Wörterbuch entstanden ist. Lies es ruhig durch, wenn dich solche Dinge interessieren!

Die **Hinweise für die Benützung** sind schon erheblich interessanter, denn sie verraten dir, was es da noch alles zu finden gibt. Es genügt, wenn du dir diese Hinweise einmal durchliest. Einige Dinge solltest du dir aber im Laufe der Zeit einprägen und merken, damit du nicht immer wieder bei den Erklärungen nachblättern musst. Dazu zählen vor allem die **Zeichen** und die **Abkürzungen**. Sie sind wie Verkehrszeichen im Straßenverkehr. Schau sie dir zunächst einmal an und schreck dich nicht, wenn du vieles nicht gleich verstehst. Wichtig ist, dass du weißt, wo du nachsehen kannst, wenn du im Wörterbuch eine Abkürzung oder ein Zeichen siehst. Aber, wie gesagt, es wäre nicht schlecht, wenn du dir die wichtigsten davon merken könntest.

Dann gibt es sicher auch ein Verzeichnis der „phonetischen Zeichen", also der **„Lautschrift",** und das **englische Alphabet**. Lies es dir einmal durch; du wird diese Zeichen immer wieder bei den englischen Wörtern im Wörterbuch finden, und es schadet nicht, wenn du weißt, was sie bedeuten.

Meist gibt es dann noch **Anmerkungen zum „Amerikanischen Englisch"**. Die Unterschiede zwischen dem Englisch in Großbritannien und in Amerika sind in der Unterstufe aber noch nicht so wichtig, sodass du diese Seiten wieder überblättern kannst, wenn dich der Inhalt (noch) nicht interessiert.

Wichtiger sind jedenfalls die **Zahlwörter und Zahlenangaben,** die in vielen Wörterbüchern angeführt werden. Die solltest du dir einmal durchlesen!

Lies das alles aber nicht an einem einzigen Tag! Lass ein paar Tage vergehen, und dann lies wieder ein paar Seiten. So merkst du dir viel mehr von dem, was du gelesen hast!

Die Maße und Gewichte, die in Großbritannien und Amerika verwendet werden, werden dir sicher gefallen. Einiges kennst du vielleicht von Aufschriften auf Getränkedosen und anderen Verpackungen aus diesen Ländern oder aus Büchern und Filmen und dergleichen. Einiges wird dir sicher neu sein. Jedenfalls verwenden die Menschen dort ein etwas anderes System zur Bezeichnung von Maßen und Gewichten, und du solltest dich irgendwann einmal damit beschäftigen.

Nun aber zum Hauptteil, dem **Wörterverzeichnis**:

Wir nehmen an, du besitzt ein Wörterbuch mit zwei Wörterverzeichnissen in einem Buch: **Englisch-Deutsch** und **Deutsch-Englisch**. (Größere Wörterbücher enthalten ebenfalls zwei Wörterverzeichnisse, nur sind sie meist auf zwei Bände aufgeteilt.)

Du wirst bei vielen englischen Wörtern sehen, dass nicht nur ein deutsches Wort daneben steht, sondern mehrere. Ebenso wirst du umgekehrt bemerken, dass bei einem deutschen Wort auch mehrere englische angegeben sind. Das erschwert natürlich die Benützung eines Wörterbuches, denn **nicht jedes Wort** der einen Sprache bedeutet auch **nur ein einziges Wort** in der anderen Sprache.

Dazu gleich ein heiteres Beispiel. Es ist nicht ganz ernst zu nehmen, aber es zeigt doch die Schwierigkeiten im Umgang mit dem Wörterbuch auf. Dies ist die Geschichte:

> Einem Touristen in einem englischen Hotel ist kalt, weil es in seinem Zimmer zieht. Er möchte eine zweite Bettdecke und droht, falls er sie nicht bekommt, dass er aus diesem Hotel auszieht. Seine Englischkenntnisse lassen aber zu wünschen übrig, und so schlägt er einige Wörter in seinem Reise-Dictionary nach. Dann übersetzt er seinen Satz:
>
> *„Da ist ein starker **Zug** in meinem Zimmer, und wenn ich nicht noch eine **Decke** bekomme, **ziehe ich aus.**"*

Und dann kam der folgende „englische" Satz heraus:

*"There is a strong **train** in my room, and if I don't get another **ceiling, I undress.**"*

Kein Brite oder Amerikaner würde verstehen, was unser armer Reisender eigentlich sagen wollte. Wie ist das möglich? Nun, wenn du in deinem Wörterbuch nachliest, dann wirst du Folgendes finden:

„Zug"	heißt	*train*
„Decke"	heißt	*ceiling* ['si:liŋ]
„ausziehen"	heißt	undress

Das alles steht im Wörterbuch, und trotzdem ist der englische Satz völliger Unsinn. Daher nochmals die Frage: Wie ist das möglich?

☆ **„Zug"** heißt natürlich ***train***; aber nur, wenn man die „Eisenbahn" meint;
aber hier ist „Zugluft" gemeint, und das heißt auf Englisch ***draught*** [drɑ:ft].

☆ **„Decke"** heißt natürlich auch ***ceiling***; damit ist aber nur die „Zimmerdecke" oder der „Plafond" gemeint. Unser Tourist aber hätte eine ***blanket***, eine Decke zum Zudecken, gebraucht!

☆ Besonders daneben ging aber das Wort **„ausziehen"**, denn ***undress*** heißt „sich ausziehen, sich entkleiden", was der Tourist hoffentlich nicht vorhatte. Er hatte „ausziehen" im Sinne von „umziehen", „das Hotel wechseln" gemeint; das heißt aber ***move*** oder ***move out*** oder ***leave the hotel***.

Richtig übersetzt hätte der Satz also lauten müssen:

*„There is a **draught** in my room, and if I don't get another **blanket**, I'll **move out.**"*

Und die Moral von der Geschicht'?

Du solltest **nicht** gleich **das erste Wort**, das du liest, **verwenden**! Du musst alles lesen, was das Wörterbuch zu deinem gesuchten Wort sagt. Das Wörterbuch irrt sich nicht – eher schon der Benutzer!

Wenn du dann dein Wort gefunden hast, solltest du eine **Kontrolle** durchführen!

Und die geht so:

> **!** Du nimmst das englische Wort, das du im „deutsch-englischen" Wörterverzeichnis neben dem deutschen Wort gefunden hast, und schlägst es im englisch-deutschen Verzeichnis nach. So kannst du feststellen, ob das gefundene englische Wort im Deutschen etwa die Bedeutung hat, die du im Sinn hattest.

Diese Kontrolle kostet zwar etwas Zeit, aber:

- ☆ Du lernst dabei viel mehr Englisch.
- ☆ Du machst beim Suchen viel weniger Fehler.
- ☆ Du lernst, wie man mit einem sehr wichtigen Hilfsmittel umgeht. Das wird dir in den höheren Klassen, wo du das Wörterbuch bei den *tests* meist verwenden darfst, von großem Nutzen sein.

Auf den letzten Seiten des Wörterbuches findest du meist eine Liste mit den ***irregular verbs***, den „unregelmäßigen Verben" der englischen Sprache. Du solltest zwar die wichtigsten kennen und auch beherrschen, aber trotzdem kann man ja – nur so zur Kontrolle – einmal nachsehen.

Wie du siehst, enthält dein Wörterbuch **viele wichtige und nützliche Dinge**, von denen die meisten Schüler gar nichts wissen! Du weißt es aber; also mache auch gut und reichlich Gebrauch davon!

Viel Spaß bei der Arbeit mit dem ***dictionary***!

BECKENACHTEN UND ARMKREISEN

Du fühlst dich schlaff?

„Male" mit deinem Becken eine Acht, damit dein Körper Energie zum schöpferischen Träumen bekommt:
Du stehst mit leicht gebeugten Knien, die Füße sind hüftbreit auseinander. Du streckst die Arme nach hinten und verschränkst die Daumen ineinander. Nun machst du mit den Hüften eine Vor- und Rückwärtsbewegung, sodass daraus eine Acht entsteht. Der Oberkörper bleibt dabei aufrecht, die Atmung ist fließend. Achte darauf, dass die Ellbogen möglichst gestreckt bleiben.

Wiederholung der Übung: 30-mal

Eine letzte Übung zur Aktivierung deiner Energie:

Du stehst hüftbreit, die Knie locker. Du kreist nun mit beiden Armen gleichzeitig von vorne nach oben, über den Kopf nach hinten.
Achte darauf, dass die Ellbogen gestreckt bleiben.

Wiederholung der Übung: 50-mal

TESTS

Englisch ist ein sogenanntes „aufbauendes" Fach. Das heißt, dass du alles, was du lernst, auch noch später beherrschen und anwenden musst. Ein * bedeutet „Stoff von früher" (5. oder 6. Schulstufe) oder „Wiederholung".

Die Punktewertung ist immer die gleiche:

46–43 Punkte = Sehr gut
42–38 Punkte = Gut
37–32 Punkte = Befriedigend
Unter 32 Punkten = Arbeite die fehlerhaften Stoffgebiete noch einmal durch!

Good luck! You can do it!

1st test

conditions ("if"-sentences)	comparison of adjectives*
questions	irregular verbs (all forms)

1. Find the correct forms of the adjectives. **12 Punkte**

a) Mount Everest is the (high) mountain on earth. It is much (high) than Mt. Blanc.
b) 10 $ is (little) than 10 £, but (much) than 10 DM.
c) What was the (exciting) film you've ever seen? – "The Phantom of the Opera". I think no other film is as (exciting) as this one.
d) I'm sorry, but I have no (far) information for you.
e) Where's the (near) petrol station? – In Bank Street, but it's closed today. The (near) one is in Canal Street.
f) Let's run! The 11:35 is the (late) train today.
g) What do you like (good), coke or juice? – Juice! I like apple juice (good) of all.

2. Find the missing forms of these irregular verbs.

12 Punkte

		feel			lie
lost				grew	
	taken		caught		

3. Conditions (I): Put the verbs into the correct tense.

6 Punkte

a) If I knew Joe's address, I (write) him a letter.
b) We will have a picnic soon if it (not rain).
c) If Nick missed the bus, we (leave) without him.
d) If you don't listen to me, you (be) sorry.
e) Our team would win the game if they (play) better.
f) Nancy would buy new skis if she (have) more money.

4. Conditions (II): Finish the following sentences in the correct tense.

6 Punkte

a) If Simon finds us here, . . .
b) If I were you, . . .
c) If Sandra was at home, . . .
d) Jack would come to my party if . . .
e) I would show you my stamp collection if . . .
f) The girls will sing for us if . . .

5. Ask for the <u>underlined</u> words and/or do the task in (. . .).

10 Punkte

a) <u>George</u> often helps <u>us</u> with the crossword puzzle.
b) Tim told <u>Aunt Mary</u> about the accident, but not his mother. (negative why-question)
c) "Star Wars" is a <u>fantastic</u> film.
d) The children bought their mountain bikes at "Sports Unlimited". (negative question)
e) The <u>early</u> bird catches the worm. („Morgenstund' hat Gold im Mund.")
f) <u>Theo and Paula</u> don't smoke <u>because it is dangerous and expensive</u>.

2nd test

modal verbs
past tense and past perfect tense
sentence connecters*
reported speech
personal pronouns*

1. Fill in the correct modal verbs from the box.

10 Punkte

be (not) allowed (2x) – may – must not (2x) –
need not (2x) – had to – should – should not

a) You . . . work outside during a thunderstorm. It's too dangerous.
b) We . . . park here. The sign says "No parking!"
c) You . . . do as much sports in winter as in summer.
d) Putting up a tent (= ein Zelt aufstellen) . . . in the town park.
e) This is the last bus today. We . . . miss it!
f) Tell Judy she . . . practise the piano today if she doesn't want to.
g) Our TV broke down yesterday. So we . . . take it to the shop.
h) You . . . make the beds today, Mark. I've done it for you.
i) Grandma says she . . . spend Christmas with us again.
k) When I was younger, I . . . stay up very late on Christmas Eve.

2. Sentence connecters*: Fill in the correct words from the box.

10 Punkte

and – because – but – so – that – when – who

a) We left the cinema . . . the film was so boring.
b) When dad came home last night he had dinner . . . then he watched TV.
c) It was dark in the old house . . . we were not afraid.
d) My brother and I always go snowboarding . . . we are on winter holiday.
e) Last year there wasn't enough snow, . . . we stayed at home.
f) William bought some eggs and flour . . . he wanted to bake a cake.
g) I know a girl . . . has met Bon Jovi.
h) The children were so tired . . . they went to bed at once.
i) . . . the rain stopped, we went outside . . . played football.

3. Past tense and past perfect tense: Fill in the correct tenses.

10 Punkte

a) After Fred (finish) his model plane, he (start) working on a motorboat.
b) Mary (not want) to be alone after she (see) the horror film.
c) The boys (go) out to play because it (stop) raining.
d) Yesterday, on the way home from school, I (find) a wallet full of £ 10 notes. Somebody (lose) it in the park.
e) Mum (cook) dinner before the guests (arrive).

4. Reported Speech: Put the verbs into the correct tense.

10 Punkte

a) Peter said, "I can't remember where I've put my watch."
b) Gina said, "We will come again next week."
c) Father said, "Bring me a hammer from the garage, please!"
d) The announcer said, "The race is going to start in five minutes."
e) Doris said, "I know why I don't like football."
f) Uncle Frank told us, "I sold my Harley-Davidson yesterday."

5. Personal pronouns: Fill in the correct words.*

6 Punkte

a) Look, there are Tim and Cathy. . . . are in my class.
I like . . . very much.
b) Carla is my best friend . . . always have a lot of fun together.
c) Jim and I are going to the sports centre. Do you want to come with . . . , Simon?
d) My sister lives in the USA now, but I often talk to . . . on the phone.
e) Have you seen Charlie? I can't find . . . anywhere.

3rd Test

past tense: simple or progressive?
present perfect tense or past tense?
some or any?*
reflexive pronouns
"The Magic Bike"

1. Past simple or progressive? Find the correct words.

10 Punkte

a) The Blacks (sit) in their living room when someone (knock) at the door.
b) I (do) my homework when my sister Laura (come) home from school.
c) When Monica (return) from her holiday, all her friends (wait) for her at the airport.
d) First I (buy) some paper and then I (paint) a nice picture of my dog.
e) While dad (read) the paper, the children (play) with their Lego-blocks.

2. Present perfect tense oder past tense?

10 Punkte

a) My aunt is a writer. She (write) six books and one play so far.
b) (you, see) Terry yesterday? He (not be) at school.
c) What (you, do) to yourself? You look different!
d) Look, somebody (put) toilet paper in my school bag. That's not funny!
e) (you, ever, be) to the USA? – No, but my family and I (go) to Canada last year.
f) When Andy (be) a child, he (hate) sport. Now he (win) the championship. Isn't that great?

3. Reflexive pronouns or not? Fill in the correct words.

10 Punkte

a) Do you like this vase, Uncle Joe? I've made it . . . .
b) "Do-it . . ." is often cheaper than buying things in a shop.
c) Nobody wanted to come with us, so we went by . . . .
d) Who told you about Martin's accident? – Martin . . . . I spoke with him yesterday.
e) Do you remember . . . Josephine? She's my cousin from France.
f) Who has built this boat? – Frank and Jack. They did everything . . . .
g) Do you sometimes ask . . . why you have to work so much?
h) I don't feel . . . well today. I think I've got a temperature.
i) Grandma lives with us now because she doesn't like living by . . . .
k) Charlie is a big problem. He doesn't know what to do with . . . .

4. "The Magic Bike" (I): Find the right connecters.

5 Punkte

a) The girl and the lady came into the shop . . . they wanted to buy a bike.
b) But they left the shop . . . they heard how much work it would take to make the old bike look new.
c) The two brothers did not want to work so much, either, and . . . they did not buy the bike.
d) The old bike was rusty and some parts were missing, . . . I liked it and . . . I bought it.

5. "The Magic Bike" (II): Right or wrong? If wrong, please correct.

5 Punkte

a) The storyteller worked for the old man in the bike shop.
b) The girl's favourite colour was pink.
c) The old man said, "You have to clean the bike and remove the old paint before you can use it."
d) It was a magic bike because it could do things other bikes could not do.
e) One day the bike was stolen and the storyteller did not get it back.

6. "some" or "any"? Find the correct words. (*)

6 Punkte

a) This is a terrible place. Let's go . . .where else.
b) Listen to me! I've got . . .thing to tell you.
c) I'll never love . . .body but (= außer) you!
d) Is there . . . milk left? – Yes, there's . . . in the fridge.
e) Dad is looking for his car keys again. Has . . .body seen them?

4th test

passive voice
modal verbs
questions and negation*

relative pronouns
present perfect simple or progressive, since or for?

1. Passive voice (I): Find the correct tenses.

6 Punkte

a) Most people think that the clock tower of the British Parliament (call) "Big Ben", but in fact it's the name of the bell, not of the tower.
b) More than 50 churches (build) after the Great Fire of London in 1666.
c) Tourists from all over the world can (find) in London.
d) In the past, the Tower of London (use) as a prison.
e) Along the Thames many of the old buildings (replace) by new ones. (to replace = ersetzen; regular verb).
f) The Globe Theatre (open) some time next year.

2. Passive voice (II): Change from active to passive.

6 Punkte

a) Thousands of tourists visit Madame Tussaud's every year.
b) Look, they have cleaned the walls of Westminster Abbey!
c) The Prince of Wales will open the new wing of the Air Force Museum in September.
d) During the Second World War, they hid many pictures and statues in the tunnels of the Underground.
e) You can see animals from all over the world at London Zoo.
f) You can't hear Big Ben this summer because they are repairing the mechanism of the clock.

3. Relative pronouns: Fill in who, that, which or nothing.

8 Punkte

a) The lady . . . opened the first wax museum in London came from Paris.
b) Did you see the sights . . . we talked about in our English lessons?
c) The statue . . . stands in the centre of Piccadilly Circus shows the Greek god Eros, . . . was the God of Love.
d) Most of the pictures . . . you can see in the National Gallery were painted by British artists.
e) What's the name of the big ship . . . is moored (= verankert) opposite the Tower? – That's H.M.S. Belfast.
f) That's the friendly policeman . . . helped us when we were lost.
g) "The Hard Rock Café" offers the best music . . . you can get in London.

4. Present perfect tense: simple or progressive, since or for?

10 Punkte

a) That's the oldest house in our town. It (stand) there . . . 1406.
b) (you, see) the Miller's new house? It's very big.
c) They (live) in it . . . two or three months now, I think.
d) Rita (not do) her homework yet, but she wants to go out and play.
e) Judith is not here. She (go) to town with her mum.
f) We (wait) for you . . . an hour. Where (you, be)?

5. Modal verbs: Fill in the correct tenses.

10 Punkte

a) I'm sure Mr Daniels would help us if he (can).
b) Doris and I went to the party, but Jenny (not, may) come along because she is too young.
c) Our car is making funny noises. We (must) take it to the mechanic some time next week.
d) Bill (can) jump over the fence if he didn't have this bandage on his knee.
e) Our old TV did not work so we (must) get a new one.
f) I don't think we (may) to see the play if we had asked our parents.
g) You (can) see the sea from your hotel if you went to the roof.
h) My dad (can) ride a bike since he was three years old.
i) You (must) try harder if you want to play on the team again.
k) I (may) stay out longer at weekends since my thirteenth birthday.

6. Questions, questions, questions.

6 Punkte

a) The concert will be conducted (= dirigiert) <u>by Sir George Solti</u>.
b) Martina doesn't like German <u>because it's a very difficult language</u>.
c) <u>David and Michelle</u> have sold their flat in London. (negative question)
d) The Smiths will invite <u>us</u> to their party next weekend.
e) Marion is waiting <u>for Daniel</u>.

5th test

tenses
possessive pronouns*
reported speech

1. Past tense: simple or progressive?

12 Punkte

a) Jean (walk) home from music school when suddenly she (hear) footsteps behind her.
b) Adrian (drive) along the river when he (lose) control over his car and (crash) into a tree. Luckily he (not, be) hurt.
c) When the stranger (enter) the bar, some men (stand) around, (talk) and (drink) beer.
d) What (you, do) at 5 o'clock this morning? – At 5? I (sleep), of course.

2. Past tense or past perfect tense?

10 Punkte

a) After the last guests (leave), we (put) the dirty dishes into the dishwasher and (clean) the rooms. Some time later Herbert (call) and (say) that Suzanne (forget) her purse somewhere in our house. We (find) it on the sofa, behind a pillow.
b) When mum (notice) the happy smile on my face, she (know) that I (pass) the exam. She (tell) me that she (think) of me a lot all day.

3. Present tense, present perfect tense or past tense?

10 Punkte

a) Jill, (you, tidy) up your room yet? – Yes, mum, I (do) it last night.
b) Dad (drive) the same car for six years, but now he (want) a new one.
c) Mum, I think I (lose) my new pen. I (look) for it for an hour, but I can't find it. – When (you, see) it last? – This morning, at school.
d) Look, there's Mike. He (ride) his bike today. Yesterday he (go) to school by bus. He usually (take) the bus in the morning.

4. Put into reported speech (reporting verb in past tense).

10 Punkte

a) "We saw a very boring play last night."
b) "Please bring me a hammer from the garage."
c) "Don't sit on your desk!"
d) "Do you know my cousin Albert?"
e) "Why didn't you ask your father?"

5. Possessive pronouns.*

4 Punkte

a) Cindy, is this . . . pullover? – Let me see. Yes, it's . . . .
b) These aren't . . . jeans. I've got "Levi's" and these are "Lee's". But ask Melanie. I think they are . . . .
c) Look, there are Kevin and John in a brandnew car. Is it . . . ? – No, it belongs to . . . parents.
d) Mr and Mrs Jacobs: "We like . . . new house very much. It has four bedrooms and two bathrooms."
Mr and Mrs Bellows: ". . . is not so big. We've only got two bedrooms."

6th test

all tenses
comparison of adjectives
"dangerous" words
conditions
"The Christmas Present"

1. Conditions (I): Find the correct tenses.

8 Punkte

a) We would have left without you if you (not call).
b) What (you, do) if somebody gave you £ 1000?
c) If we (go) to bed earlier, we would not be so tired all the time.
d) I (not wear) running shoes with a skirt if I were you.
e) If Mr Simmons knew that you didn't do your homework by yourself, you (must) do it again.
f) If I (know) what it was, I wouldn't have eaten it.
g) (you, invite) Charlie and Mac if you hadn't met them before?
h) If we had not put on our raincoats, we (get) wet to the skin.

2. Conditions (II): Finish these sentences in the correct tense.

4 Punkte

a) If we had played better, . . .
b) They would have opened the door if . . .
c) Would you have come if . . . ?
d) . . . if you had stayed longer?

3. Comparison of the adjective: Find the correct forms.

12 Punkte

a) Take an umbrella with you. The clouds are getting (dark) and (dark).
b) Many young people like videos (good) than books, but I think active reading is usually (interesting) than passive watching.
c) "(near), please!" the doctor said, but nobody wanted to go.
d) The holiday was (cheap) than we thought, so we spent (little) money than we had planned.
e) Riding a motorbike is much (dangerous) than driving a car. – Yes, that's true. And it is getting (expensive) and (expensive), too.
f) The (big) the house, the (heavy) the work.
g) Meeting you here was (surprising) thing that happened to me.

4. "Dangerous" words: Choose the correct ones.

6 Punkte

a) The pictures we saw of the earthquake (= Erdbeben) were really shocking / shocked.
b) There were hundreds of terrifying / terrified children and grown-ups running around in the ruins.
c) Toby is only nine years old, but he is very much interesting / interested in physics.
d) It is amazing / amazed how much he knows about stars and atoms.
e) If you find this book boring / bored, I can give you a different one.
f) Tanya was so exciting / excited that she could hardly speak.

5. All known tenses: Find the correct form of the verbs.

8 Punkte

a) While we (wait) for the beginning of the show, loud music (come) from the loudspeakers.
b) After Fanny (go) home, Matthew (be) very sad.
c) Fanny and Matthew (know) each other for two years now. They (become) good friends.
d) Yesterday we (must) take Norman to the hospital because he (swallow) Mum's hairpin. (to swallow = schlucken; hairpin = Haarnadel)

6. "The Christmas Present": True of false?

(Read the story before you do the exercise, not while you are doing it!)

8 Punkte

a) Pamela and Abdi were in the same class at school.
b) Abdi's parents did not like Pamela and told Abdi not to go out with her.
c) Pamela's grandmother was living with them.
d) Pamela and Abdi lived in different parts of the town.
e) Pamela's present for Abdi was a CD with classical music.
f) Abdi could not read and write although he was fifteen years old.
g) Pamela's grandmother taught Abdi to read and write.
h) Pamela was happiest about Abdi's present.

UNREGELMÄSSIGE ZEITWÖRTER

IRREGULAR VERBS

Die **drei Grund- oder Stammformen des Zeitworts** sind:

base form (infinitive)	–	Nennform, Infinitiv
past form (past tense)	–	Mitvergangenheit, Präteritum
3rd form (past participle)	–	Mittelwort der Vergangenheit

Es folgt eine Liste wichtiger *irregular verbs.* Solltest du ein großes Englisch-Deutsch-Wörterbuch besitzen, dann wirst du darin eine umfangreichere Liste finden. Die Formen der folgenden *verbs* solltest du dir im Laufe der 7. Schulstufe gut einprägen.

TIPP

Noch ein Tipp zum Lernen:
Irregular verbs folgen keiner Regel. Es gibt auch kein System, nach dem du dir die Stammformen leichter merken könntest. Daher solltest du gleich beim Vokabellernen immer alle drei Formen „einstudieren“:

„singen“ heißt dann eben nicht *sing,* sondern *sing – sang – sung* usw.

A

base form (infinitive)	past form (past tense)	3rd form (past participle)	Deutsch
to be	was/were	been	sein
to beat	beat	beaten	schlagen
to become	became	become	werden
to begin	began	begun	beginnen
to bite	bit	bitten	beißen
to blow	blew	blown	blasen, wehen
to break	broke	broken	brechen
to bring	brought	brought	bringen
to build	built	built	bauen
to burn	burnt	burnt	brennen
to buy	bought	bought	kaufen
to catch	caught	caught	fangen
to choose	chose	chosen	wählen
to come	came	come	kommen
to cost	cost	cost	kosten
to cut	cut	cut	schneiden
to do	did	done	tun, machen
to draw	drew	drawn	zeichnen, ziehen
to drink	drank	drunk	trinken
to drive	drove	driven	fahren (selbst)
to eat	ate	eaten	essen
to fall	fell	fallen	fallen
to feel	felt	felt	fühlen
to fight	fought	fought	kämpfen
to find	found	found	finden
to fly	flew	flown	fliegen
to forbid	forbade	forbidden	verbieten
to forget	forgot	forgotten	vergessen
to freeze	froze	frozen	frieren
to get	got	got	bekommen
to give	gave	given	geben
to go	went	gone	gehen
to grow	grew	grown	wachsen
to hang	hung	hung	hängen
to have	had	had	haben
to hear	heard	heard	hören
to hide	hid	hidden	verstecken
to hit	hit	hit	schlagen
to hold	held	held	halten
to hurt	hurt	hurt	verletzen
to keep	kept	kept	behalten, halten
to know	knew	known	kennen, wissen

base form (infinitive)	past form (past tense)	3rd form (past participle)	Deutsch
to leave	left	left	verlassen
to lend	lent	lent	leihen
to let	let	let	lassen
to lie	lay	lain	liegen
to lose	lost	lost	verlieren
to make	made	made	machen
to mean	meant	meant	bedeuten
to meet	met	met	treffen
to pay	paid	paid	bezahlen
to put	put	put	legen, setzen
to read	read	read	lesen
to ride	rode	ridden	fahren, reiten
to ring	rang	rung	läuten
to rise	rose	risen	sich erheben
to run	ran	run	laufen, rennen
to say	said	said	sagen
to see	saw	seen	sehen
to sell	sold	sold	verkaufen
to send	sent	sent	schicken
to shake	shook	shaken	schütteln
to steal	stole	stolen	stehlen
to shine	shone	shone	scheinen
to shoot	shot	shot	schießen
to show	showed	shown	zeigen
to shut	shut	shut	schließen
to sing	sang	sung	singen
to sit	sat	sat	sitzen
to sleep	slept	slept	schlafen
to speak	spoke	spoken	sprechen
to spend	spent	spent	verbrauchen
to take	took	taken	nehmen
to teach	taught	taught	lehren
to tear	tore	torn	(zer)reißen
to tell	told	told	erzählen (+object)
to think	thought	thought	denken, glauben
to throw	threw	thrown	werfen
to wake	woke	woken	aufwachen, wecken
to wear	wore	worn	tragen (Kleidung)
to weep	wept	wept	weinen
to win	won	won	gewinnen
to write	wrote	written	schreiben

Versetzung gefährdet – was nun?
Rechtlicher Rahmen und Aufgaben der Eltern in Deutschland

Wenn die Versetzung eines Kindes gefährdet ist, sind auch seine Eltern gefordert. Auf jeden Fall ist es sinnvoll, dass Schule und Elternhaus dieses Problem gemeinsam erörtern, nach den Ursachen fragen und nach Abhilfe suchen. Sie als Eltern sollten nicht nur über den rechtlichen Rahmen zur Leistungsbeurteilung und Versetzung informiert sein; Sie sollten auch wissen, was Sie selbst unternehmen können, um das festgefahrene Schiff wieder in besseres Fahrwasser zu lenken.

Rechtlicher Rahmen
Auskunft über die jeweils gültigen Rechtsvorschriften zur Leistungsbeurteilung und Versetzung können Eltern in den Amtsblättern und dem Staatsanzeiger nachlesen, die bei jedem Schulleiter sowie dem Schulamt einzusehen sind.
Da für jedes Bundesland eigene Vorschriften existieren, möchte ich die Ausgestaltung des rechtlichen Rahmens am Beispiel des Hessischen Schulrechtes (Quelle: Dienst- und Schulrecht Hessen, GEW-Handbuch, völlig neu bearbeitete Ausgabe, Stand März 1994) erörtern.
Wird eine Leistung im Zeugnis mit schlechter als der Note „ausreichend" bewertet, so entscheidet die einfache Mehrheit der **Versetzungskonferenz** über die Versetzung oder Nichtversetzung der Schülerin oder des Schülers. Zur Teilnahme ist jeder Lehrer, der die Schülerin oder den Schüler im laufenden Schuljahr oder vor einem Lehrerwechsel unterrichtet hat und wer die Schülerin oder den Schüler vor einem Lehrerwechsel im laufenden Schuljahr zuletzt unterrichtet hat und noch der Schule angehört, verpflichtet (a.a.O., Abt. 5, § 12,2):

> *„Die Versetzungsentscheidung wird aus **pädagogischer Verantwortung und frei von Schematismus getroffen**. Grundlage sind die Leistungen und die Entwicklung der Schülerin oder des Schülers während des ganzen Schuljahres (a.a.O.; Abt. 5, § 11,2)."*

Verschlechtert sich die Schülerin oder der Schüler in einem Fach von einem auf das nächste Schulhalbjahr, so ist dies von der Fachlehrerin oder dem Fachlehrer in der Versetzungskonferenz zu begründen.
Verlauf und Ergebnisse der Versetzungskonferenz werden im **Protokoll** festgehalten, welches jederzeit von den Eltern eingesehen werden kann.

> *„Eine Note schlechter als ausreichend in einem Fach oder Lernbereich kann nur durch die Note befriedigend oder besser in einem anderen Fach oder Lernbereich ausgeglichen werden (a.a.O., Abt. 5, Anlage 1; 11,2)."*

Zusätzlich gilt für Schülerinnen und Schüler an Gymnasien und Realschulen: Schlechter als mit der Note „ausreichend" beurteilte Leistungen in einem der Fächer Deutsch, erste Fremdsprache (für Gymnasiasten auch die zweite Fremdsprache) und Mathematik hindern eine Versetzung dann nicht, wenn die Schülerin oder der Schüler **besondere Fähigkeiten und starken Arbeitswillen** in einem anderen dieser o.g. Fächer oder in mehreren anderen Unterrichtsfächern erkennen lässt. Dies könnte unter Umständen durch die Note „befriedigend" gegeben sein.
Mehr als zwei mit schlechter als der Note „ausreichend" beurteilte Leistungen in den Fächern Deutsch, erste Fremdsprache (für Gymnasiasten auch die zweite Fremdsprache) und Mathematik können in der Regel nicht ausgeglichen werden (a.a.O., Abt. 5, Anlage 1).
In den Jahrgangsstufen 7 bis 10 ist eine **nachträgliche Versetzung** möglich:

„Wird eine Schülerin oder ein Schüler auf Grund schlechter als ausreichend bewerteter Leistungen im Zeugnis in zwei Fächern oder Lernbereichen nicht versetzt, so kann die Versetzungskonferenz die Schülerin oder den Schüler zu einer ***Nachprüfung*** *in einem der zwei Fächer oder Lernbereiche innerhalb der ersten sechs Unterrichtstage des neuen Schuljahres dann zulassen, wenn bei schlechter als ausreichend bewerteter Leistungen in nur einem Fach oder Lernbereich die Versetzung möglich gewesen wäre (a.a.O., Abt. 5, § 16,3)."*

Aufgaben der Eltern
Einfühlungsvermögen und Kommunikationbereitschaft sind grundlegende Eigenschaften von Eltern, die bereit sind, sich frühzeitig mit schulischen Misserfolgen ihres Kindes auseinander zu setzen.
Eltern mit solchen Grundeinstellungen sind eher in der Lage, Warnsignale rechtzeitig zu erkennen, um ihrem Kind in schwierigen Schulsituationen rechtzeitig zu helfen.

Ist die „Fünf" in der Klassenarbeit ein Ausrutscher oder schon ein Warnzeichen?

Suchen Sie dazu das **sachliche Gespräch mit Ihrem Kind**, um gemeinsam über Gründe des Misserfolges nachzudenken und nach Lösungen zu suchen!
Darüber hinaus kann ein **Gespräch mit der unterrichtenden Lehrerin oder dem unterrichtenden Lehrer** zu wichtigen Erkenntnissen führen. Die Sprechstunden der Lehrerinnen und Lehrer während des Schuljahres werden kaum wahrgenommen. Das Gespräch wird meistens dann gesucht, wenn es bereits „zu spät" ist.

Bei **anhaltenden Misserfolgen** müssen sich die Eltern fragen:

Ist mein Kind in dieser Klasse mit dem jetzigen Lernstoff überfordert?

Langfristige Überforderungen führen in der Regel zu psychischen Verletzungen des Kindes; ständige Misserfolge kratzen am Selbstwertgefühl und wirken demotivierend. Die Familienatmosphäre ist zumeist auch in Mitleidenschaft gezogen.
Dabei sollte es das Ziel der Eltern sein, ihrem Kind aus der Zone der Misserfolge herauszuhelfen, damit es bei Erfolgen wieder Lob und Anerkennung erfahren kann.
Dazu könnte unter Umständen die **Änderung des Schul- und Ausbildungsweges** erforderlich sein. Vielleicht nimmt aber schon ein **rechtzeitiges Zurückgehen** Ihres Kindes in die vorhergehende Jahrgangsstufe den störenden psychischen Druck.

Sollte eine schlechte Note auf kurz- bzw. mittelfristig zu schließende Lücken oder Defizite im lernmethodischen Bereich zurückzuführen sein, können – bei Bereitschaft des Kindes – **außerschulische Förderungsmaßnahmen** (z. B. Lernhilfen, Nachhilfe, Kurse „Das Lernen lernen") sinnvoll bzw. erfolgreich eingesetzt werden.

Hedi Jantsch
Vorsitzende des Schulelternbeirates
am Friedrichsgymnasium Kassel

„Nicht genügend"! Was können Eltern dagegen tun?

Pädagogische Aspekte und rechtliche Situation in Österreich

Der pädagogische Beurteilungsspielraum

Die Bestimmungen des Schulunterrichtsgesetzes über die Leistungsbeurteilung an den Schulen zielen einmal darauf ab, ein höchstmögliches Ausmaß an Objektivität zu gewährleisten, sind doch oft sehr wesentliche Berechtigungen an das Bestehen oder Nichtbestehen einer Prüfung geknüpft. Andererseits wird auch der Umstand berücksichtigt, dass eine Leistungsbeurteilung in der Schule immer auch eine pädagogische Maßnahme ist. Es würde sich eher ungünstig auf die Motivation der Kinder auswirken, wenn der nachlässige Schüler auf Grund seiner Begabung leicht zu guten Beurteilungen kommen würde, der strebsame Jugendliche aber immer nur eine unerfreuliche Beurteilung erhalten könnte. Jeder würde im Laufe der Zeit seine Bemühungen einstellen, wenn er sähe, dass er das gewünschte Ziel niemals erreichen kann. Oder umgekehrt, warum sollte sich ein begabtes Kind anstrengen, wenn es auch ohne jede Mühe Anerkennung fände. Das Schulunterrichtsgesetz hat daher dem Lehrer in einigen Bereichen einen „pädagogischen Beurteilungsspielraum" eingeräumt.

Ein Lehrer wird diesen vor allem dadurch nützen, dass er die Mitarbeit des Schülers im Unterricht, seine Bemühungen bei der Anfertigung der Hausaufgaben – so wie es im § 3 der Verordnung über die Leistungsbeurteilung festgelegt ist – gleichwertig in die Gesamtbeurteilung einbezieht. Hier hat der Lehrer die Chance, ausgleichend, motivierend, ermutigend die Leistungsbeurteilung mit seinem pädagogischen Auftrag zu verbinden. Es wäre pädagogisch unklug und widerspräche den Bestimmungen des Schulunterrichtsgesetzes, wenn nur die Schularbeiten zur Leistungsbeurteilung herangezogen würden.

Die Informationspflicht des Lehrers

In engem Zusammenhang mit diesen Bestimmungen ist die vorgeschriebene Transparenz zu sehen. Eine pädagogische Maßnahme kann nur dann eine günstige Auswirkung haben, wenn der Schüler Informationen darüber erhält, inwieweit es ihm gelungen ist, Leistungen nachzuweisen, etwa bei der Wiederholung oder Erarbeitung neuer Lehrstoffe. Positive Rückmeldungen in diesem Bereich werden auch den schwachen Schüler veranlassen, sich lebhaft am Unterricht zu beteiligen, was sich im Allgemeinen längerfristig auch positiv auf die Ergebnisse der Schularbeiten auswirken wird.

Der Lehrer ist verpflichtet, Aufzeichnungen im erforderlichen Ausmaß anzufertigen, Schüler und Eltern haben ein Recht auf Transparenz.

Was darf geprüft werden?

Grundsätzlich darf nur das geprüft werden, was im Lehrplan steht (Schulbücher gehen oft weit über die Anforderungen des Lehrplans hinaus!) und was bis zum Prüfungszeitpunkt durchgenommen wurde.

Die Benotung

Bei der Festsetzung einer Note für ein gesamtes Schuljahr hat der Lehrer alle im Laufe des Jahres erbrachten mündlichen wie schriftlichen Leistungen (nicht Leistungsbeurteilungen) zu berücksichtigen. Die viel geübte Praxis, einfach eine Durchschnittsnote zu bilden, entspricht nicht den Bestimmungen des Schulunterrichtsgesetzes, schon gar nicht, wenn dazu nur die Ergebnisse der Schularbeiten herangezogen werden. Es geht vielmehr darum, am Ende des Schuljahres zu beurteilen, ob der Schüler durch seine Leistungen gezeigt hat, dass er das, was im Unterricht durchgenommen wurde (und was auch im Lehrplan vorgesehen ist), wenigstens überwiegend kann. Wie und bei welcher Gelegenheit, ob im Rahmen der mündlichen Mitarbeit, etwa bei der Lösung einer Aufgabe an der Tafel oder bei einer

Schularbeit oder bei einer mündlichen Prüfung, Leistungen nachgewiesen wurden, ist dabei unerheblich. Alle erbrachten Leistungen müssen gleichwertig herangezogen werden.

Ein Lehrer wird eine Leistung mit **„Gut"** oder **„Sehr gut"** beurteilen, wenn ein Schüler über das Wesentliche hinaus oder weit über das Wesentliche hinaus Leistungen erbringt.

Ein Lehrer wird eine Leistung mit **„Befriedigend"** beurteilen, wenn der Schüler den Anforderungen in den „wesentlichen Bereichen" entsprochen hat. Ein **„Genügend"** signalisiert hingegen, dass der Schüler in den „wesentlichen Bereichen" Lücken hat. Er hat den Anforderungen nur überwiegend entsprochen. Gerade in den so genannten aufbauenden Gegenständen, in denen der neue Lehrstoff auf Vorkenntnissen aufbaut, kann das fatale Folgen haben. Hat zum Beispiel das Kind in der Unterstufe des Gymnasiums in Mathematik nur lückenhafte Kenntnisse erworben, sind Schwierigkeiten in der Oberstufe fast vorprogrammiert. Ein „Genügend" genügt also nicht immer! Der Lehrer wird Auskunft darüber erteilen, wo diese Lücken sind und wie man sie möglichst schnell schließen kann.
Ein **„Nicht genügend"** erhält ein Schüler dann, wenn es ihm nicht gelungen ist, den Anforderungen in den „wesentlichen Bereichen" wenigstens überwiegend zu entsprechen. Was sind nun die so genannten „wesentlichen Bereiche"? Das Bundesministerium für Unterricht und Kunst vertritt hier die Meinung, dass ein Lehrer dies im Laufe des Unterrichtsjahres selbst zu definieren hat. Es ist jedenfalls nicht zulässig und widerspräche dem Grundsatz der Transparenz, erst nach einer Prüfung zu sagen, was wesentlich und was unwesentlich gewesen wäre. Gegen ein „Nicht genügend" bei einer Schularbeit oder bei einer Prüfung können Eltern keine Berufung einlegen, auch wenn diese Note als ungerecht empfunden wird. Ein Schüler, der sich über eine verpatzte Schularbeit ärgert, hat jedenfalls das Recht, sich einmal im Semester in jedem Gegenstand zu einer mündlichen Prüfung zu melden.

Meinem Kind droht ein „Nicht genügend".
Was soll ich tun?
Für Eltern ist es wichtig zu analysieren, worauf ein so umfangreiches Versagen des Kindes zurückzuführen ist. Hat nur das eigene Kind versagt oder der größte Teil der Klasse? Hat das Kind sich mit dem nötigen Fleiß vorbereitet oder nicht? Haben vorübergehende physische oder psychische Probleme zu einem eher einmaligen Versagen geführt? Zu einer objektiven Klärung der Ursachen führt in erster Linie ein Gespräch mit dem zuständigen Lehrer, auch ein Kontakt mit anderen Eltern der Klasse kann hilfreich sein. Führt dies nicht zu einer befriedigenden Antwort, kann die kostenlose Hilfe des schulpsychologischen Dienstes in Anspruch genommen werden. Durch entsprechende Tests kann der Schulpsychologe herausfinden, ob das Kind in einer seiner Begabung entsprechenden Schule ist, oder ob ein Schulwechsel auf Grund der Begabungsrichtung für das Kind nicht besser wäre.
Eltern mögen bedenken, dass sich hinter einem so genannten „faulen Kind" nur allzu oft ein Schüler verbirgt, der den Anforderungen nicht genügen kann oder dies jedenfalls von sich selbst glaubt. Es ist oft weniger diskriminierend, faul als dumm zu sein. Eine rasche Klärung und eine vernünftige Reaktion der Eltern werden dem Schüler helfen, ein gesundes Selbstwertgefühl aufzubauen. Schulische Erfolge werden sich so viel leichter einstellen.
Kein Kind mit einem „Nicht genügend" fühlt sich besonders wohl. Auch ein Schüler, der seine Pflichten versäumt hat, benötigt Hilfe und Informationen, wie die Lücken geschlossen werden können, Hilfe bei der Zeitplanung und bei der Beschaffung von Lernunterlagen, mit denen das Kind selbstständig arbeiten kann. Lob und Anerkennung für die ersten kleinen Erfolge helfen dem Kind mehr als Vorhaltungen. Ein Nachhilfelehrer sollte nicht gleich bestellt werden, kurzfristige Erfolge könnten längerfristig dazu führen, dass sich ein Kind an Hilfe gewöhnt und womöglich zu dem Ergebnis kommt, dass es alleine zu guten Leistungen nicht fähig ist.
Sollten alle Schüler einer Klasse mehr oder weniger nur genügende oder nicht genügende Leistungen erbringen, und sollte dies wiederholt geschehen, ist der zuständige Elternvertre-

ter aufgerufen, mit dem Lehrer und – wenn dies nichts fruchtet – auch mit der Schulaufsicht Kontakt aufzunehmen. Einerseits kann auf Dauer nicht hingenommen werden, dass den Schülern nur lückenhafte Kenntnisse vermittelt werden können, andererseits sind negative Auswirkungen auf die Motivation zu befürchten. Die Schüler könnten „lernen", dass alle Anstrengungen doch nur zu einer schlechten Beurteilung führen, und in ihrem Fleiß nachlassen.

Was soll mein Kind tun?

Meldet sich ein Schüler bei einem drohenden „Nicht genügend" zu einer mündlichen Prüfung, wird ihm der Lehrer die Gelegenheit einräumen, Leistungen in den „wesentlichen Bereichen" nachzuweisen, wo dies dem Schüler bislang nicht möglich war. Eine umgekehrte Vorgangsweise wäre schikanös und anfechtbar. Wenn es dem Schüler gelingt, zu den bisher erbrachten Leistungen, die für ein „Genügend" noch nicht ausreichten, zusätzliche Leistungen nachzuweisen, wodurch die Anforderungen in den „wesentlichen Bereichen" nunmehr überwiegend erfüllt werden, so ist ein „Genügend" zu erteilen.
Bei allzu großen Lücken, die im Laufe eines ganzen Jahres entstanden sind, wird es aber eher aussichtslos sein, im Rahmen einer einzigen mündlichen Prüfung, deren Dauer auf 10 bzw. 15 Minuten begrenzt ist, nachzuweisen, dass alle Lernrückstände aufgeholt wurden. Schüler neigen dazu, allzu große Hoffnungen auf diese letzte Prüfung zu setzen. Nur bei einem geringen Rückstand besteht die Möglichkeit einer Notenkorrektur.

„Nicht genügend". Kann mein Kind trotzdem aufsteigen?

Grundsätzlich sind Schüler mit einem „Nicht genügend" nicht zu einem Aufsteigen in die nächste Klasse berechtigt. Ganz im Sinne seiner pädagogischen Ausrichtung sieht das Schulunterrichtsgesetz jedoch eine wichtige Ausnahme vor.
Hat der Schüler nicht bereits im vorigen Jahr im gleichen Gegenstand ein „Nicht genügend", und ist dieses Fach weiter im Lehrplan vorgesehen, kann die Klassenkonferenz, in der alle Lehrer vertreten sind, die in der Klasse unterrichten, beschließen, den Schüler aufsteigen zu lassen. Voraussetzung für eine positive Entscheidung ist, dass die Leistungen in allen anderen Fächern so gut sind, dass der Schüler aller Voraussicht nach im kommenden Jahr erfolgreich am Unterricht teilnehmen kann.
Der Gesetzgeber geht hier davon aus, dass die Leistungsreserven eines Schülers begrenzt sind. Die Lehrer einer Klasse müssen gemeinsam eine Prognose darüber abgeben, ob ein Schüler die Lücken in einem mit „Nicht genügend" beurteilten Gegenstand bei fortschreitendem Unterricht im folgenden Schuljahr angesichts der Situation in den anderen Fächern wird aufholen können:
Wie viele mit „Genügend" beurteilte Gegenstände enthält das Jahreszeugnis?
Hat ein solches „Genügend" eher eine Tendenz zum „Nicht genügend" oder zum „Befriedigend"?
Reichen die Kenntnisse in einem mit „Genügend" beurteilten Fach aus, oder müssen auch hier erst Lücken geschlossen werden, um dem Unterricht im kommenden Schuljahr folgen zu können. (Ein schwaches „Genügend" steht einem Aufsteigen in die nächste Klasse dann nicht entgegen, wenn zum Beispiel in Geographie Kenntnisse in Gesteinskunde fehlen, im nächsten Jahr aber die Wirtschaftsräume auf dem Programm stehen.)
Hat ein ansonsten zufrieden stellend arbeitender Jugendlicher aus besonderen Gründen (zum Beispiel Scheidung der Eltern, schwere Erkrankung) nur vorübergehend nachgelassen und steht zu erwarten, dass er leistungsstark genug ist, die Defizite aufzuholen?
Die Lehrer werden auf Grund ihrer Erfahrung und ihres Sachverstandes zu einer vertretbaren, sinnvollen Lösung kommen.

Die Berufung

Eltern können gegen die fehlende Berechtigung zum Aufsteigen in die nächste Klasse berufen und dabei das „Nicht genügend" und die Entscheidung der Klassenkonferenz anfechten. Aussichten für eine erfolgreiche Berufung sind dann gegeben, wenn Eltern bei einem „Nicht genügend“ darlegen können, dass sachfremde Gründe, etwa disziplinäre Schwierigkeiten, bei der Beurteilung eine Rolle gespielt haben, die geforderten Kenntnisse aber sehr wohl vorhanden sind. Es ist sicher nicht einzusehen, dass in einem solchen Fall ein Kind nur wegen seines unangenehmen Verhaltens ein ganzes Jahr wiederholen soll. Manchmal können auch reine Formfehler eines Lehrers dazu führen, dass ein „Nicht genügend“ aufgehoben wird. Lehrer sind keine Juristen und sollten es wohl auch nicht sein. Ein so erfochtener Erfolg ist in der Regel kein Erfolg für das Kind. Die Lernrückstände des Kindes werden so nicht geschlossen, und ein vertrauensvolles Klima der Zusammenarbeit zwischen Eltern, Lehrern und dem Schüler könnte nachhaltig gestört werden.

Gegen den Beschluss der Klassenkonferenz könnte erfolgreich eingewandt werden:

– dass außergewöhnliche Belastungen des Kindes nicht berücksichtigt wurden, besonders, wenn gegen Ende des Schuljahres wieder eine steigende Tendenz erkennbar war;

– dass die fehlenden Kenntnisse in einem mit „Genügend“ beurteilten Fach im folgenden Jahr keine Rolle mehr spielen oder nicht grundlegend für das Verständnis des Lehrstoffes im kommenden Schuljahr sein werden. Nicht erfolgreich sind meistens Berufungen, die sich auf einen Notenvergleich mit anderen Schülern beziehen.

Berufungen sind formlos. Ein einfacher Brief an die Schule genügt, in dem zum Ausdruck gebracht wird, dass man gegen die Nichtberechtigung zum Aufsteigen in die nächste Klasse beruft und das „Nicht genügend“ und (oder) den Beschluss der Klassenkonferenz nicht für gerechtfertigt hält. Die Chancen steigen mit einer möglichst sachlichen Begründung. Die Schule leitet die Berufung an den Landesschulrat weiter. Dieser kann entweder auf Grund der vorgelegten Unterlagen entscheiden oder, wenn diese nicht ausreichen, kurzfristig eine kommissionelle Prüfung unter dem Vorsitz eines Schulaufsichtsbeamten durchführen. Der gesamte Jahresstoff kann Gegenstand einer solchen Prüfung sein. An dieser Stelle sei noch einmal darauf hingewiesen, dass das wichtigste Kriterium für eine Berufung die abgesicherte Überzeugung der Eltern sein sollte, dass das Kind über die erforderlichen Kenntnisse verfügt.

Gegen die Entscheidung des Landesschulrates ist eine Berufung beim Bundesministerium für Unterricht und kulturelle Angelegenheiten möglich. Es kann sinnvoll sein, wenn eine auch räumlich weiter entfernte Behörde die Angelegenheit noch einmal prüft. Immerhin werden im Schnitt ca. 25% der dort eingelangten Berufungen positiv entschieden.

Ingrid Buschmann
Pressesprecherin des Bundesverbandes der Elternvereinigungen an Höheren und Mittleren Schulen Österreichs

Die Durchstartübungen

DIE LEHRE

Die Übungen beruhen auf der Kinesiologie, der Lehre von der Bewegung. Sie unterstützt alle deine Tätigkeiten – auch dein Lernen. Durch die Anwendung bestimmter Bewegungsmuster kannst du deine Möglichkeiten voll ausschöpfen.

DER AUTOR

Kim da Silva lebt in Berlin. Er studierte Chemie, Physik, Botanik, Mikrobiologie und Lebensmittelchemie. Nach fünf Jahren als Assistent an der Freien Universität Berlin und sechsjähriger Forschungsarbeit in der chemischen Industrie arbeitete er viele Jahre in einem pharmazeutischen Weltkonzern.

In seiner Jugend reiste er viel und erwarb sich sein Wissen um die verschiedenen Philosophien und Heiltraditionen.

In den 70er Jahren lernte Kim da Silva die Kinesiologie kennen.

Er war einer der Ersten, die bei Dr. Paul Dennison eine Ausbildung in Edu-Kinestetik erhielten. Heute zählt er zu den wenigen europäischen Ausbildnern für Edu-K-Teacher.

Von Kim da Silva sind bereits einige Bücher erschienen.

DIE AUTORIN

Do-Ri Amtmann, geboren 1958, von Beruf Drogistin, lernt und lehrt seit 1985 mit Kim da Silva. Seit 1988 leitet sie ein Kinesiologie-Zentrum in Baden und die Edu-K-Teacher-Ausbildung für Österreich.

Kim da Silva & Do-Ri Amtmann freuen sich, wenn du ihnen von deinen Übungserfahrungen schreibst. Sie werden dir gerne antworten und auf Wunsch auch mehr Informationsmaterial über ihre Arbeit zusenden.
Schreibe an:

Kinesiologie-Zentrum
Do-Ri Amtmann
Lamprechtgasse 7
A-2500 Baden

Kim da Silva
Türkenstraße 15
D-13 349 Berlin 65

STICHWORTVERZEICHNIS

active voice 34, 61
adjective 94, 101, 154
Bedingungssätze 67
Beifügung 49, 59
besitzanzeigendes Fürwort 77
bezügliches Fürwort 108
Bitte (indirekte Rede) 89
conditional perfect 45, 55, 69, 81
conditional present 45, 55, 81
conditions 67, 144, 145, 154
dictionary 138
direct speech 81, 82
direkte Rede 81, 82
Eigenschaftswort 94, 101
Entscheidungsfrage 84
Ergänzungsfrage 87
Frage 10, 13, 27, 40, 49, 84
Fürwort 108
future perfect tense 81
future progressive 27
future tense 27, 37, 45, 54, 81
Gegenwart 9, 12, 13
Hilfszeitwort 40, 44, 45, 55
if-sentences 67
indirect command 89
indirect speech 39, 74, 81, 82
indirekte Frage 84
indirekte Rede 39, 74
indirekter Befehl 89
ing-form 12
irregular verbs 144, 145, 156
Leideform 34
„man"-Sätze 41
modal verbs 45, 146, 150, 151
negation 49, 150
negative Frage 57, 58
Objekt 35, 40, 49, 111
passive infinitive 44
passive progressive 42, 43
passive voice 34, 62, 150
past participle 9, 10, 29, 34, 44
past perfect tense 29, 37, 39, 45, 54, 69, 80, 146, 147, 152
past tense 9, 11, 12, 17, 20, 43, 45, 78, 79, 80, 147, 148, 152
personal pronoun 41, 75, 79, 112, 146, 147
persönliches Fürwort 41, 75
possessive pronoun 76, 77, 79, 152, 153
Prädikat 35
present participle 12, 27, 37
present perfect progressive 12, 13, 16, 17, 150, 151
present perfect simple 10, 11, 12, 16, 17, 150, 151
present perfect tense 9, 16, 37, 45, 54, 80, 148, 152
present tense 9, 13, 43, 45, 75, 79, 152
progressive form 9, 15, 20, 27, 42, 55, 148
pronoun 108
question 49, 84, 144, 150, 151
reflexive pronoun 117, 118, 148
Reizwörter 11
relative clause 113
relative pronoun 108, 110, 112, 113, 150
Relativpronomen 108
Relativsatz 113
reported question 84
reported speech 39, 74, 146, 147, 152
rückbezügliches Fürwort 117, 121
"self"-pronoun 117, 119, 123
simple form 9, 15, 20, 148
some and any 149
Steigerung 94, 96, 99, 100, 144
Subjekt 10, 13, 34, 35, 41, 111
Tätigkeitsform 34
tenses 61, 75, 79, 152, 154
verb 9
Verbot (indirekte Rede) 89
Vergangenheit 9, 12
Vergleich 94, 103, 104, 105, 154
Verneinung 10, 13, 27, 40, 49
Vorvergangenheit 29
Wörterbuch 138
Zeitstufen 61, 77, 78
Zeitwort 9, 15, 35
Zukunft 27